health-conscious participants from all over the country. The instructions for it were fairly simple: remove toxic and stressful foods and replace them with highly nutritious ones, a lot of water and important nutritional supplementation.

"I was a bit skeptical about how successful I would be because my work keeps me on the road a lot, and it is difficult to find healthy food while traveling, especially fresh juices. But Scott's ideas have always shown me a clear, simple way to get the most from a personal wellness regime. I resolved to do the best I could.

"Much to my surprise, after three weeks of literally pigging-out on vegetarian soups, casseroles, smoothies, and fresh organic munchies, I had a very positive report. I had lost an average of two pounds a week, no longer needed a caffeine kick at the end of a long day, and I couldn't care less if I ever crossed paths with anything containing sugar. But, best of all, when I looked at my blood under my microscope (called Live Cell Analysis) I had no aggregations (clumps of blood cells that are stuck together). My blood had never looked better.

"I have learned more about realizing a healthy existence from Scott than I ever learned in nursing school. Healthy people are happy people and fun to be with. I encourage any person interested in feeling better to try out this inner 'spring cleaning' and enjoy the results."

Keli MacIntosh, Registered Nurse,
Certified Nutritional Consultant

"One of my most empowering results I received after Scott's cellular cleansing program is being face to face with food that looks good, smells good and probably tastes good, but I can now say, "No," because I know how I will feel an hour later, tomorrow or even two weeks later. I no longer want to put those

clogging foods into my body.

"Another unexpected benefit has been in how others react to me. Deep down, I believe that everyone realizes that a cleansing diet would be beneficial. They just want to see someone they know doing it! I'm watching my hard-core junk food friends eliminating sugar, dairy, and changing what they intrinsically know doesn't work anymore.

"Take it at your own pace. Do what is right for you. There is an online support forum so you never feel alone. This cleanse really helps you make the choices you've wanted to all along, because your taste buds end up choosing for you."

Joann Tomasulo

"For most of my adult life, I have experienced Irritable Bowel Syndrome-type symptoms. I became used to having cramping, bloated feelings after eating almost anything.

"I also developed extreme joint pain which often left me debilitated for hours each day. When I woke up in the morning, I had so much excruciating pain in my feet and lower legs that it was usually too difficult to stand in the shower. I would typically soak in a hot tub for the first 15 minutes to loosen up my feet. I often felt like my toes were curled under and I couldn't stand flat.

"I had a skin tag next to my eyebrow which was initially diagnosed as a wart. A dermatologist removed it using a scalpel. It bled profusely but eventually healed without scarring. Within 18 months, it was back and looked pretty scary. The dermatologist wanted to biopsy it this time, so out came the scalpel again. This time, for good measure, I had to go in weekly for several weeks to have acid applied to make sure it was really gone. Sure enough, within 18 months it was back once again. Never once was a diet or cleansing connection mentioned.

"Twenty four hours after starting the cleanse outlined in this book, the Irritable-Bowel symptoms were gone. This is after years and years of having the symptoms.

"For the first time in over ten years, I have had a significant reduction in pain and other symptoms such as feeling somewhat dizzy or otherwise 'off balance'. I now sleep much better and have more energy.

"My skin has gone through a transformation. The skin tags completely disappeared. I also had a rash on my knee for approximately 4 years; I had been told that it was probably a version of a yeast infection. This too disappeared after about a week on the cleanse.

"My understanding of illness and food have changed in a very significant way. While my joint pain and other symptoms had been very real, I began to understand that my body had not been nourished in a way where it could heal. I began to have a sense that my body would function very well if only I would provide the nourishment it needed so very much. Since I experienced such significant results so quickly, that sense was confirmed literally within days of starting the cleanse. My body had not been doing anything wrong - my symptoms were simply a manifestation of the body's struggle to "do the right thing." It has been very hard to explain to family and friends as I've talked with them about the success of this process - it now seems such a natural, right thing, that I can't imagine how others wouldn't grasp these ideas.

"It is amazing how quickly and completely our bodies will rebound and respond once it has a chance to clean out and be fed highly nutritious food."

Karen Ackley Tredwell

Published by:
Genetic Press
Longmont, CO

First Edition: July 2002
Second Edition: April 2003
Third Printing: May 2004

Printed by:
Thomson–Shore, Inc.
www.tshore.com

Library of Congress Cataloging-in-Publication Data
Ohlgren, Scott, 1956–
Cellular Cleansing Made Easy: regenerate your health without giving up food, sex, or sanity.

ISBN: 0-9721483-2-9

CELLULAR CLEANSING MADE EASY

Regenerate Your Health Without Giving Up Food, Sex, or Sanity.

Join hundreds of others nationwide on the next
28-day online cellular cleansing program.
www.HowHealthWorks.com

SCOTT OHLGREN

Contents

PART 1:
WHERE WE ARE, AND HOW WE GOT HERE — 31

10

The next great advance in the health of the
American people will come not from hospitals or laboratories, but from what people
learn to do for themselves.

Dr. Norman Shealy, MD

Introduction

Cleansing. So What?

<<:::>><<:::>><<:::>><<:::>><<:::>><<:<<:::>><

From Susie Richardson, Registered Dietitian

As a Dietitian since 1980, I have worked in clinics, hospitals, and nursing homes. If you want to see your probable future, go visit these places. It is a harrowing experience. Given what I now know about the diet/disease connection, I can't help but wonder how dietary changes, including the cleansing program outlined in this book, could have prevented some of the suffering I observed.

When I was nineteen, I began eating a vegetarian diet that replaced meat with eggs and dairy foods. Whole grains, occasional beans, vegetables, and plenty of cheese and yogurt were the mainstay of my diet, and just to make sure, I took vitamin and mineral supplements to cover all bases. My caloric intake was right on target for my age and activity. By all accounts I should have been in the best of health. I wasn't. I gained weight. My skin looked uneven and blemished. I was often bloated. I craved sweets. The monthly PMS and mood swings became unbearable. My exercise endurance was low. What was I missing? Did I need more vitamin supplements?

I first encountered the concept of internal cleansing in 1982 when I attended a lecture by someone who claimed that what we eat could not only prevent illness, but also reverse it. I was fresh out of college, a nutrition degree in hand. I knew that some of what I had been taught was politically flavored, and I wanted to know what else was out there.

What I learned at this lecture changed my life. But first it changed my way of looking at food, my body, and how what we eat can create our condition, be it health and vitality, or illness and disease. I learned about traditional foods and cultures, how through the ages our food has changed in such a way that what once was nourishing food, now had become depleting and even disease-promoting. I learned how what I had been eating just might be the cause of most, if not all, of the symptoms I was experiencing. I discovered how the body is self-healing and how foods can help to cleanse and clear away the muck that has resulted from growing up in a generation raised on toaster pastries, pasteurized and homogenized beverages, and soda pop.

I was brought up on the Standard American Diet. You know the one, "The Four Basic Food Groups." It included: white bread, canned and processed foods, plenty of sugar-sweetened cereal, lots of milk for calcium and meat for protein. This, we were taught, built strong bodies and vibrant health. I knew I had some un-learning to do.

I immediately went home and cleared out my refrigerator. I was so motivated that I didn't even mind giving away the yogurt and cheese, my two favorite foods. I took out my new recipes and went to the natural food store and stocked up on more organic vegetables and fruit, whole cereal grains and beans. My refrigerator and cabinets welcomed some new staple items that I still use today, including miso, sourdough bread, olive oil, and unrefined salt. My cleansing journey had begun.

Within a few days I began to notice changes. I found that I needed a lot more sleep at first. I was assured that this was because as the body starts to clear out, it requires extra energy to do so. Later on I went through a stage of frequent urination, another sign of cleansing. The most notable—and for me the most convincing—sign that what I was doing was working, was that my skin temporarily became what I will refer to as an oil slick. All those years of cheese and ice cream (I was the dairy queen!) were coming undone. My self-healing body was purging all of that yuk, and it was wonderful.

But here's the good news: *I never experienced another bout with PMS.* I lost the puffiness in my face, that baby fat look which comes from sugar and dairy food; my mood swings subsided, I lost weight, had more energy and endurance, lost the chronic bloating. During that first Spring, I began coughing. And coughing. It lasted for several weeks. There was no fever. I was not sick. My body was simply clearing out all of that stored up, metabolic waste. I celebrated. It took some time, but eventually my skin cleared up and I said goodbye to my craving for sweets. To this day I eat a modified version of this, which I simply refer to as conscious eating.

Was this a big change? You bet. Was it worth it? Without question.

When I first met Scott Ohlgren we were both students of health and nutrition. I was impressed by his desire to learn and speak the truth. I noticed that Scott questioned things, and searched for his own answers. Right there we had a lot in common. His studies led him to incorporate what made sense, experience the results, and refine the methods. Writing and teaching is a natural outgrowth of his sincere desire to help others who seek to learn how to improve the quality of their health and lives. It is his passion, one he presents with contagious enthusiasm.

This 28-day program is the result of years of research and experience. I know this because I've been witness to Scott's commitment to discover and uncover the facts about health and disease. His resources are reliable. Moreover, he's done the work on himself and has supported countless others with these methods, which he presents in an intelligent, common sense, and often humorous manner.

Within these pages is a simple, powerful method for self-renewal. I mean that in the most literal sense. In this book Scott details information that will take you to your next level of well-being. You will learn how you got to the point to where you are; you will learn the mechanics of internal cleansing, and how to do it. You will choose the level of participation that feels comfortable and right for you. You will have online support, where your questions will be answered, your concerns addressed. There will be guidelines for planning ahead to make it a smooth and fun adventure. Scott has made every effort to make this workable for your lifestyle.

For the past twenty years my work has focused on teaching about nutrition and health, supporting clients with what they choose to do from what they learn. Step by step. The very fact that you are reading this book indicates that you're ready for your next big step. Congratulations. May the pages that follow be your road map towards a life of not better, but the best of health and quality of life.

Suzanne Richardson
Registered Dietitian
susier@bossig.com
208 263-9422

If we thought of cells, if we thought of
molecules, every moment, every day,
the awe would tame us.

Sybil Smith

A New Body Owner's Manual

<<:::>><<:::>><<:::>><<:::>><<:::>><<:<<:::>><

D^{ear} Reader,

Welcome, and congratulations on the decision to learn about the power of a simple, effective, working person's cleansing program. It is a decision that may well alter your life.

As those who participate in this cleanse will learn, first over a 28-day period, and then in the months that follow, the title of this book could very well be *A New Body Owner's Manual*. You might end up calling it that not because it's a nice catchy phrase, but is in fact a reference to the most underrated and misunderstood truth of human biology: that every few years, we are, no joke, a new body.

Sure, we already acknowledge this about our hair, and our fingernails, because these body parts regenerate at a speed that we can see. But did you know that the very hands you are using to hold this book are not the hands you had back in 1995? The very muscles in each of your fingers, the tendons you see, even the 27 bones in each hand—they are not the same bones that were there a few years ago. Your trillions of cells have been completely replacing themselves with new cells, new ingredients, new material.

Once you become aware of this simple regeneration fact,

and then see and feel that regeneration happening during a nutritional cleansing program, a question will start to emerge in your mind. That question is not only the central pillar, the core around which this book is written, it is also the one that I believe should lie at the center of all nutritional and disease education:

What have you been replacing those cells with?

Look now at your arms, and your face, and the overall condition of your skin. For the moment, imagine being able to see through and underneath the skin, to your muscles, your liver, your spleen. Picture your blood stream, and imagine its overall consistency and makeup. Those cells, even the ones that make up the heart currently beating in your chest, were not here a few years ago.

Give this some thought for a moment. Think about your own "organ and tissue replacement program" over the past few years and decades. If it is true that you are a new body from the one you had even five or six years ago, what have your particular replacement choices given you?

Now pose the deeper questions:

Would a higher level of nutrients, year to year, have given you a healthier, more symptom-free, more vibrantly alive body?

Over the natural course of generations, would this higher level of nutrients affect the genetic outcome of our future children's health?

Once you personally witness the changes that occur in just a 28-day period, the answers to these questions become crystal clear: *you bet. Our vitality—and our illnesses—*

stem largely from our food choices.

After 20 years of studying the relationship between food and health, of paying attention to it, of working with individuals and lecturing nationwide and being in the business that links food and health, as well as selling over 70,000 booklets, tapes, and videos on health, here is what I know for certain: our current concept of disease is incorrect. Illness does not come from "out there" but is in fact an inside job. **A change in nutritional intake can eliminate disease.** Not simply "make it better," or "improve." Real food can eliminate a diseased state. It can shrink tumors and reverse organ malfunction and slow the aging process. We become less susceptible to the cellular metabolic waste conditions currently and incorrectly referred to as "colds" and "the flu." We regain our energy. I have watched how an improved nutritional intake allows people to get off daily insulin shots, weekly cortisone pills, and hourly sniffs of "post-nasal drip" spray. I have seen how a change in nutritional intake helps a person handle stress and avoid emotional roller coasters. Even the sense of self-esteem and self-awareness can change with a shift in nutrition.

Anyone who personally witnesses these changes eventually comes to this same obvious conclusion: the large majority of every skin condition, lung problem, liver malfunction, reproductive disease, heart condition, blood/ bacteria/ fungus/ yeast/ tumor producing internal terrain mess is the result of a metabolic toxic overload, stemming directly from the life-deadening and historically new food chain we and our children are currently consuming. Any witness would conclude that endometriosis and tumors and acne are not some disease that just happens, but instead are each the *end, visual result* of a nutritional toxicity process that started a long time ago, and are as close to home as hand to mouth.

Make the indelible connection

In the forties and fifties, you could find full page ads in the most popular magazines with doctors and well-known actors promoting cigarettes as a way to "relax," "get a better disposition," and "ease sore throats." These advertisements disappeared once enough people experienced the true effects of smoking cigarettes.

Drinking and driving used to be joked about after a hard night of partying. Even among adults with social standing, it was looked upon with a wink, nudge, and a good laugh. This behavior changed once enough people had the experience of the very real horrors produced by driving drunk.

These are just two examples of a culture collectively realizing that there existed a correlation between certain behaviors and certain effects.

We are now at a similar place, where there is a desperate need for adults to make a new link of responsibility— an indelible connection between a behavior and a result. Two thirds of us are dying from our nutritional choices, not because we want ourselves and our children to suffer in this manner, but because *we do not really believe that we are responsible.*

What is missing is a personal experience of this responsibility, this "here are my food choices, and here is my condition" connection. It is time we grow up.

Who should read this book?

Cellular Cleansing Made Easy has a very specific and narrow focus: it is designed to give you enough insight into the food-illness connection so that you are motivated into action— **specifically, a 28-day action** of cellular cleansing. Remember, the main purpose here is to create a movement for nutritional sanity. This movement will not happen through intellectual discussion about the wrongs of selling McDonald's in school cafeterias. It will only happen through enough people having the physical experience—the "oh-my-god, I get it aha!" that comes from feeling the effects that our modern diet has on our health. There is no easier way to experience that than through a cell-regenerating nutritional cleansing program.

WHY A CLEANSE?

The first and most obvious reason is the health of this vehicle you inhabit. A nutritional cellular cleanse is akin to a *human body oil change*. We would never consider driving an automobile, decade after decade, without changing its oil, yet we have no concept in our culture for the need to do this to our own body vehicle. From hundreds of books and writings on natural health spanning two thousand years and scores of authors from Hippocrates to America's Dr. John H. Kellogg (yes, of corn flake fame), to the more recent Drs. Dean Ornish, Bernard Jensen, William Harris, Michael Klaper, Richard Schulze and many others, you will see references to repairing health through dietary cleanses. **There is simply no more powerful way to heal your body than through a nutritional cleansing program.** *Nothing comes close* —be it drugs, surgery, vitamin pills, expensive therapy, whatever—to its potential for cellular repair. These 28 days can build a foundation of health and vitality that most people will only dream of.

The second reason? Proof. We currently live in a time when virtually all hospitals, universities, medical professionals and other officials assigned the job of explaining the process of health to us lay people, believe that the cure to our symptoms is pharmaceutical drugs. This 28-day program has the potential to show you how painfully ignorant and untrue this belief is. The physical, emotional, and mental changes that you can experience during a simple dietary cleanse are enough to prove the diet/disease, diet/health connection.

The third reason is of a more social nature. Few people complete the cleansing and superfood program unaltered. Losing a set of symptoms through nothing but a change in *what you are putting into your mouth each day* is a transformative, eye-opening, lose-your-social-conditioning and reexamine-what-the-hell-we've-been-taught-about-health experience. And in a culture where so many think that the key to curing breast cancer is just a few billion dollars away in further drug research, and where a growing number of parents and teachers have been bilked into believing that children— our country's future leaders— learn better with behavioral modification chemicals coursing through their blood stream, this personal experience of yours can literally alter history.

The world changes when enough people have this experience—this realization—that their symptoms are the end effect, *not the cause*, and that the responsibility for health or illness lies in their food choices.

Join what is becoming a national movement of getting healthy *internally*. Learn about other participant's results at www.howhealthworks.com. Do your own 28-day internal cleanse, and then share your own experience with others. By doing so, you will play a vital role in bringing common sense and sanity back to our understanding of how health works.

Scott Ohlgren

Important Note Before Starting

UNDERSTANDING THE POWER OF CULTURAL BELIEF

Ever notice when you're driving an automobile, how there can often be a part of your vision that is blocked? Sometimes this blind spot is caused by a section of the car frame, or the mirror, or maybe it's a large truck in the road blinding the view of what is ahead.

One of the potential pitfalls of any culture is similar blind spots that prevent us from seeing life as it is. They can be caused by social conditioning, unexamined beliefs we picked up from our parents or teachers, or a large variety of other factors.

Currently, the single largest cultural blind spot—in terms of numbers killed or injured— is how we look at health. Nope, it's not drunk driving, AIDS, cigarette smoking or homicides. It is specifically in our perception of how symptoms occur on and inside our body, and where those symptoms actually come from. You need only to see one example — say, watching overweight youth suffer from the effects of diabetes—to know that this blind spot, this gap in our knowledge, is causing untold suffering and pain.

Doing a cleansing program without first understanding this deeply embedded cultural blind spot is not a good idea. It is not that you *can't* do it; it is more that your chance of succeeding and completing the program is slim, largely because of this mental training we have all received. In essence, it's the training that has us concluding that the majority of our physical symptoms are "diseases"—meaning that they rarely have anything to do with us, and we are not responsible. In a nutshell, this approach says:

"My headache stems from my body's lack of aspirin."

"My dandruff appears only because I ran out of the blue shampoo."

"I have a tumor because the damn doctor didn't give me enough chemotherapy."

"My depression is chemical [and I'm certainly not the chemist]."

I've heard this one many times: "My Crohn's Disease is incurable."

Entering the world of cellular cleansing with this approach will simply not work. As the weeks of your program progress, your body can go through changes that are too easily misinterpreted as one more symptom in need of one more pharmaceutical cure, particularly if *where we are*—healthwise and belief-wise— *and how we got here*, hasn't been examined.

Fortunately, understanding our current situation and cultural beliefs does not take a college thesis or six months of study to grasp. It's simple—this is a short book—but at the same time, it is a very important part of the process of getting back our health.

To that end, this book is divided into two parts. The first is titled, appropriately enough, *Where We Are, and How We Got Here*. Part Two is *The NACHO: The 28-day North American Clean the Heck Out Program*.

Patients storm into our offices, begging for
a quick cure with a miracle drug they've
just read about in their newspapers... they
follow the voices of televised drug
commercials and consider health
something that can be purchased in a
bottle at the drugstore; they
forget—or never knew—that health can be
found only by obeying the clear-cut laws
of nature.

Dr. Henry Bieler, MD

Doctors give drugs of which they know little, into bodies of which they know less, for
diseases of which they know nothing at all.

Voltaire

PART ONE

WHERE WE ARE, AND
HOW WE GOT HERE

"Six of the ten leading causes of death in
the United States have been linked
to our diet."

Senator George McGovern, reading from "Dietary Goals of the US"
as part of the 1977 Senate Select
Committee.

"67% of all diseases are diet related"

Surgeon General C. Everett Koop,
1988

The 67 Percentile

Read the two quotes on the opposite page, by Senator George McGovern and former Surgeon General C. Everett Koop.

Let these two statistics sink in for a moment. What are these extremely conservative sources saying? They are trying to tell us that two out of every three people that you know— those in your immediate family, those in your town, your state, your country—are either in the process of dying, or will start dying soon **because of their meal choices.** They are not dying from some unknown boogieman disease. No, they are dying by their own hand. Not suicide, but dietary suicide. What these quotes are telling us is that our current, historically very new, and unique diet is killing us. They are telling us that we have lost the relationship between what we eat and how our health actually works.

How we Americans are getting sick is not normal. Any brief review of epidemiological statistics (the study of disease within a population) shows this to us. Look at the following:

1. **The percentage of ailments has changed over time.**

- In 1900, 1 of 7 Americans died of cancer.
- In 1940, 1 of 4 Americans died of cancer.
- In 1998, 1 of 3 Americans died of cancer.
- Currently, the rate of cancer now kills over 1,400 people every day. That's one American every 55 seconds.

2. **Not everyone dies in the same way; the variety of ailments differs from one country to another.**

- The US, UK, Finland, and Sweden have the highest incidence of osteoporosis. Coincidentally, these countries consume more dairy foods than any others.
- Thailand, Philippines, and Chile populations, who consume the least amount of dairy food, have less than half the rates of osteoporosis than the U.S. Some cultures (e.g. African Bantu) are virtually free of osteoporosis. Some country's inhabitants do not get weak bones.

Chasing Symptoms

To help us understand symptoms, and how they happen, let's take a look at the biggest symptom happening in the United States: **indigestion**. We know it's big, because antacid and digestive medicines are currently the largest selling prescription drugs of all time. Interestingly, that number one slot during the 1980s was held by antidepressant drugs, but those now hold the number two position. How we went from a country that was mainly depressed, to one that is mainly gaseous is a fascinating story I would bet, but I'm going to let a psychologist or philosopher write that book. For now, let's look at how human digestion works, and see if it can give us an idea of why we are experiencing this particular problem.

The 5 Steps of Digestion

Step 1 is in food itself—whole foods have substances in them called enzymes that break down the foods in which they are found.

Step 2 is chewing—by munching up each mouthful, our teeth break down the bonds in food and allow us to get at many nutrients.

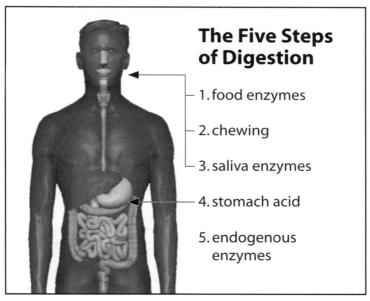

The Five Steps of Digestion

1. food enzymes
2. chewing
3. saliva enzymes
4. stomach acid
5. endogenous enzymes

Step 3 is saliva—our saliva contains many substances, mainly enzymes, that help further digest food.

Step 4 is stomach acid—often given a bad name, stomach acid is a crucial step in digestion; we would not be alive without it.

Step 5 is endogenous enzymes—endogenous simply means "of the body", so we can also call these *body enzymes.* Our body—mainly our pancreas—produces over two quarts a day of these enzymes each day.

To understand why so many people are now suffering from the body breakdowns associated with indigestion, let's actually follow a day in the life of "Digestion Dan," our modern day everyman example.

Digestion Dan

At the age of 29, Digestion Dan has a fairly fast, fairly normal lifestyle. Like all of us, his first step of digestion is food enzymes, the ones built naturally into all living things. But 97% of Dan's diet consists of highly processed foods. The things he eats have been baked, ground up, bleached for color, cooked and then dried again, reformed and mixed with other cooked and baked items, then fried in a type of oil that is designed to never spoil (called *hydrogenated*), then sprinkled with a preservative, packaged, boxed, and put on a shelf where Digestion Dan buys it five months later and takes it home where he adds water, zaps it in the microwave, and eats this meal with a drink that has been heat pasteurized to kill anything living in it, and homogenized for consistency—and because Dan has done this for the last few decades—Dan's first step of digestion is gone. There are no enzymes in processed foods.

Steps 2 and 3 of the 5 steps of digestion (chewing and

saliva) are not functioning well either. Dan gulps his food, and then washes down each meal with a diet soda.

This enzymatically dead, un-chewed, no-saliva food now drops down into Dan's stomach, where there is Step 4, stomach acid. Actually, Dan's body has quite a bit of stomach acid, because his body, over the last few decades, has been compensating for the lack of the three previous digestive steps. It does this by increasing the amount of stomach acid. This was not a bad decision for Dan's body to make. We die if we don't digest our food (picture eating a hamburger, and it just sitting at the bottom of your stomach, week after week). So, step 4 of the digestive process is not only working, it is overworking.

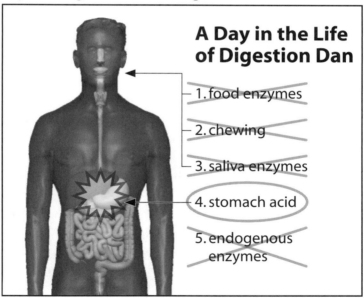

A Day in the Life of Digestion Dan

1. food enzymes
2. chewing
3. saliva enzymes
4. stomach acid
5. endogenous enzymes

Step 5, then, is Dan's body enzymes, mainly produced by the pancreas. But since the functionality of our organs is dependent on the quality of nutrition that it has been fed over the years, Dan's pancreas is not producing many enzymes these days. Having been fed mainly junk food stripped of nutrients, Step 5 is not functioning well.

Let's review: only one out of five steps in Dan's digestive process is working properly—his stomach acid.

Remember why this story is important? Because we learned that the largest health problems in America are now those associated with digestive disorders—ulcers, colitis, gas pain, heartburn, constipation, chronic diarrhea, diverticulosis, Crohn's disease, etc.—as shown by the amount of prescription and over the counter drugs taken for these conditions.

The Loss of Common Sense

Wait, we're not done. It gets better. Here is where the real insanity comes in. What do antacid medications do? **They successfully neutralize stomach acid. They *work*.** Digestion Dan's pink medicine neutralizes the stomach acid, his last remaining tool for digesting food. Congratulations, Dan. All 5 steps of your digestive process are now gone.

The pain in Dan's stomach has his attention. But now we are starting to understand something: this pain is not the real problem. The problem is what took place for that pain to occur. Aha, we get it: Dan's symptoms are simply the end result of a dietary process that began a long, long time ago.

Digestion Dan is not a fictitious character; he is everywhere. As a matter of fact, according to the Senate's dietary goals report and Dr. Koop, he is 67% of everyone in America. Two out of every three people you know.

Furthermore, Dan's digestive-related symptoms are not the only symptoms that have a direct causal relationship to food. The vast majority of illnesses have their roots in what we are eating, yet most are being 'repaired' with their assigned version of the pink pill.

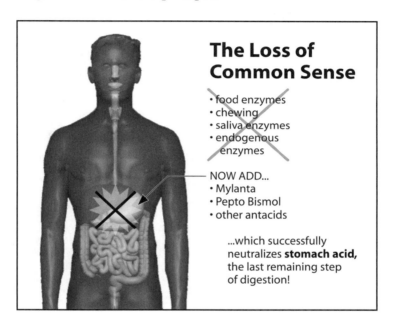

We have lost our common sense. We have quite literally lost our roots, our understanding of how closely linked our health is to our daily bread. Because of this, we, along with our medical profession, have completely confused "getting rid of symptoms" with "curing the problem."

In my opinion, one of the major injustices—really, crimes— happening in America today is this belief: "Here, take the little pink pill and you can eat any kind of junk you want." Where do they sell Pepto Bismol? At the grocery store checkout stand! Retailers are thinking, "Hey, based on what is in your cart, yeah, you'll need some of this."

Dr. Andy Tutino

The 3 Challenges to Our Inner Terrain

What, then, are the central reasons for our loss of health? Why are 67% of us dying from our own food choices? The answer is not difficult. It can be found by looking at the nutritional elements critical for health, but now missing in our modern day food chain. As you'll see, these elements play a key role in our overall condition—our *inner terrain*—and we need to learn ways of putting them back. Let's start by looking at the three challenges to this inner terrain. They are:

1. Empty Harvest, Empty Soil
2. Toxic Load
3. Poor Digestion

1. Empty Harvest, Empty Soil

The name of this first challenge to our inner terrain comes from a book titled *Empty Harvest*, by Dr. Bernard Jensen and Mark Anderson, who describe what has happened to our farm soil since World War II. The authors demonstrate, through analyses of soil samples taken in the U.S. in the 1930s and then again a few decades later, that the amounts of minerals and vital nutrients present in the soil have severely declined over time.

We have all been taught that spinach is a good source of iron. This is not the case any more, or more accurately, it depends. It depends on the soil in which the spinach has been grown.

Essentially, foods have 3 to 70 times less nutritional value than they did in the 1940s (The Baer Report, Rutgers University, 1948, 1963). To put this in perspective, it can take us up to 70 bowls of spinach to get the same amount of iron, zinc, and other micronutrients that our grandparents would have received from just one bowl.

MINERALS ARE KEY

What's the big deal with minerals anyway? Aren't minerals simply rocks in the ground? That's precisely what they are. The shiny zinc metal you see in tin cans is an element on the Periodic Table that we all studied back in eighth grade…and it's needed in every cell of your body in *infinitesimal* amounts.

The iron in bridges and carpenter nails, along with copper, chromium, manganese, chlorine, boron and approximately 80 of the 103 elements found in the earth's crust are nutrients that we need in our blood and tissues in order to operate well. Zinc boosts mental function and plays a role in taste, smell, and moods; boron is needed to convert Vitamin D, help alleviate bone loss, and plays a role in estrogen activation; manganese is needed for our brain; if the body is missing chromium, the pancreas cannot manufacture the hormone insulin. The tissues are unable to grab the sugar from the blood. And on and on, through each of these 80+ elements. It's as if we humans needed a small amount of topsoil in us to survive. Dr. Linus Pauling, one of the few people to ever win two Nobel Prizes, said it this way, *"You can trace every sickness and ailment to a mineral deficiency."*

Here's a statement directly from a USDA document: *"Plants do not manufacture minerals; they absorb them from the soil."*

Why is this relevant? It reminds us that if the nutrients are not in the soil, then they're not going to be in the vegetables. If they are not in the vegetables, then they are not in us.

2. Toxic Load

The second challenge to our inner terrain is what could be called *Toxic Load*. We are all familiar with the concept of toxins. We know, for instance, that some chemicals and pesticides, or certain fumes we breathe, can be toxic to us.

What is new is learning that many of our modern day food choices can create a toxic environment that slowly lowers our overall immunity. The phrase Toxic Load refers to the condition of our cells and tissues—the *inner terrain*— that develops when we consume, year after year, highly processed foods.

Since the 1940s, there have been over 15,000 invented food products created for the marketplace. Most of these are made up of highly processed substances. Very few resemble the original plant or animal from which they came.

Many of these foods build up a toxic residue —a sludge factor—in our bodies. This sludge does not digest well, it taxes our energy and Immune System, and it leaves something behind. This residue has a highly detrimental effect on inner terrain, our overall condition.

Imagine taking a cone filter and pouring slightly dirty oil through it. What happens? At first the oil is successfully cleaned by the filter. Eventually, though, the filter reaches a point where its ability to function slows down. It gets clogged, and the oil starts to back up and overflow. You have reached saturation.

This is what happens inside our bodies. A diet high in processed food creates a similar sludge and saturation. Welcome to the world of symptoms.

There are a variety of reasons why hydrogenated oil and bleached white flour (to pick 2 of the 15,000) are more difficult to digest, and create more sludge in our bodies, than eating the entire whole wheat grain and cold pressed olive oil. One of the biggest reasons though, and the one that plays a large role in turning around health, is enzymes.

ENZYMES ARE KEY

Enzymes are the tiny, microscopic parts of life that act as a catalyst. They are necessary in every biological process, from the beating of a heart, to the breakdown of food. There are tens of thousands of different kinds of enzymes, present in everything that lives, from trees, to soil, to digestive tracts.

We need enzymes to digest. Without them, foods do not break down well. Eat an apple and all the enzymes in that apple help digest that apple. Everything carries its own set of enzymes.

Here's the problem: processing kills enzymes; so does heat over 115 degrees or so. Remember, most of the 15,000 new foods are processed, heated, baked, denatured, and then cooked again; thus, they're completely devoid of enzymes. Here is where the toxic load, aka the *sludge factor*, enters.

Does this mean that all cooking is bad? Of course not. Every long living, sustained society in the world cooks much of their food, and many have better longevity records than we do. More importantly, most of those cultures are not coming down with the varieties and numbers of symptoms that we are now seeing in our own society.

Many foods (squash and kale, for instance) would be difficult to digest without heat. And cooking can actually make some nutrients more available for digestion.

Understanding the role of enzymes isn't just about eating raw foods. It does mean, though, that somewhere in our food preparation, we must replenish the enzymes that have been lost.

3. Poor Digestion

The third main challenge to keeping a strong inner terrain and health is poor digestion. The two biggest ways that we create bad digestion are:

1. By regularly eating foods that are devoid of enzymes, the "life spark." The resulting sludge created in the intestinal tract makes a perfect growing medium for a host of bad bacteria.

2. By regularly adding antibiotics, chlorinated and fluoridated water, stress, most prescription drugs, and excessive sugar. All of these decrease beneficial bacteria and increase harmful bacteria.

"Well, wait," some people ask, "if I don't have constipation or diarrhea, why would bad bacteria be a concern to me?"

Ask anyone who has ever had a Candida or yeast condition, for instance, how they feel when their body is filled with yeast and bacteria that don't support human life. They will give you a large list of symptoms, like muscle and joint pain, skin problems, headaches, even reproductive issues, depression, and on and on and on.

It is estimated that the annual cost of treating bacterial infections in the US alone is approaching $5 billion per year (that's $13 million per day, $560,000 per minute, $9,000 per second). We spend $400 million annually on laxatives. Over 40 percent of the 140,000 Americans diagnosed with colon and rectal cancer die each year (that's 165 deaths a day). There are now over 100,000 *colostomies* performed each year (275 a day). A colostomy is a surgical operation that creates an artificial anus through a new opening made in the stomach. There is only one reason that these people need a second anus: it is because the pathway to their first one rotted out from fecal sludge and waste. There is no other reason.

Fifty five thousand Americans die each year from this fecal sludge and waste disease, also known as colon cancer. Another forty thousand will die from sludge and waste of the stomach.

These numbers now represent the highest per capita rate of digestive tract deaths in the world. The sale of adult diapers has gone through the roof. More adults in America walk around with a diaper under their dress or suit than any other country in the world. All of this without a hint of shock or irony, as if incontinence were just a natural part of getting older.

FRIENDLY BACTERIA ARE KEY

One of the main keys to preventing this kind of internal sludge is friendly bacteria, also known as friendly micro-flora, or *probiotics*. As you'll learn—and witness through a cleansing program—our physical and mental sanity depend on having an internal environment where friendly bacteria thrive. They are the interface between life out-side, and life inside. We are not sterile environments, and friendly bacteria are how we maintain this interface.

Bacteria neither create nor control their
environment. Bacteria multiply and grow in
the environment in which they find themselves. This environment is determined by
the host.

You may perceive the intruders as "bad",
creatures of malice that must be destroyed.
Actually, they are not bad; they are merely
in the wrong place for our needs. By keeping your body fit through diet, you will be
able to peacefully coexist with germs.

Dr. Ted Morter, author of
Your Health, Your Choice.

The 4 Steps to Cellular Regeneration

So what is the key to living a long, healthy life? One of the main answers lies in a simple, biological truth: we are a self-regenerating organism.

What does this statement mean? Simply, that our body is constantly in the process of rebuilding itself. Each cell lives its life span and eventually expires. These expired cells are then flushed out and replaced with new cells.

Depending on what source you read (from Dr. Deepak Chopra, to *Gray's Anatomy*), our body replaces its tissues and cells every 1 to 7 years.

- Muscles every 6 months to 3 years
- The pancreas every 5-12 months
- Our bones every 8 months to 4 years

- Red blood cells every 90-120 days
- The intestinal lining every 5-30 days

Keep in mind, we have been doing this regeneration every day since the day we were conceived.

Once we fully understand that this replacement has been occurring, and is occurring, the question becomes, "What is the best way?" And, "Okay, I want to experience this regeneration for real. I want to see the benefits that can occur in my own body—better skin, lessening of symptoms, more energy, more mental clarity ... how long does that take and what is the easiest way?" There are four steps:

Step #1 -
Stop the Toxic Load

No amount of great nutrition in the world will work very well until our body stops receiving the massive amounts of processed and outright fake foods that create such a toxic inner terrain. We are capable of killing ourselves with many of the food products we are consuming.

Fortunately, it's easy to learn what is hard on your body; no complex charts to memorize. Rule One: the more processed a substance is, the larger the toxic load. Simply examine your weekly intake. Isolate the top 3 to 5 processed food items—these are the ones getting in the way of your goals. Slow them down. Eat less of them. Find healthier substitutes. Or, drop them altogether. We'll show you how in the cleansing program.

Step #2, 3, and 4 - The Three Rs

Three of the steps to rebuilding powerful health also happen to be the exact solutions to the 3 Challenges, mentioned earlier. They are:

1. Re-Mineralize
2. Re-Bacterialize
3. Re-Enzymize

Think of these as the "3 Rs" from old school days. Teachers knew that if students had "Reading, 'wRiting, and aRithmetic" skills, they would have the foundation on which all future education could be built.

RE-MINERALIZE

The easiest, most effective way to remineralize your body tissues is through finding and using the world's most **mineral-dense whole foods.**

Contrary to what vitamin manufacturing and marketing companies have assured us, human mineral needs have never been about gross amounts. You can consume a handful of supplements that proudly state "50,000 Units in each capsule!", or buy the upgrade to "500,000 Units!", but that has **absolutely nothing** to do with whether you will absorb and utilize those units. The amount of minerals that we need is so minuscule (millionths of a gram), it is seldom a question of "getting enough." It is an issue of absorption.

This is why we don't suck on a carpenter's nail at the first signs of anemia. If you've ever eaten vitamin and mineral supplements created from rock dust, or chemically chelated in a laboratory, and then seen the color of your urine the next morning (bright, almost neon yellow), you know that we don't digest minerals and vitamins very well that way. Perhaps most importantly, isolated mineral supplements cannot duplicate the synergy of nature, the crucial and complex relationship between each component. In his book, *Empty Soil, Empty Harvest*, Dr. Bernard Jensen gives an example: *"If inorganic cobalt is missing in the soil, the plant cannot absorb it and convert it to organic cobalt. Without organic cobalt, the human body cannot manufacture vitamin B12. When we don't get enough vitamin B12, we can't assimilate iron properly or make strong red blood cells; we become anemic, depressed, and vulnerable to disease."*

Diet/disease researcher Dr. Lynne August, MD, puts it this way: *"Yes, minerals are 'natural'; however, a mineral is not organic until it has been incorporated into an organic matrix. This organic matrix combines the mineral with carbon, hydrogen and oxygen. These complex matrices are made by **microorganisms in the soil.**"*

Statements like these are everywhere in research literature, and they indicate clearly why **plant life** is still the finest way to absorb minerals and micronutrients. **We need that translation process**, created so elegantly by their root and absorption systems. The key then, especially during this cleansing program, is consuming the soil and water-based plants that have been grown in mineral-rich environments. The two most reputable sources that you will see recommended throughout this book and the cleansing program are 1) organic vegetables, and 2) sea and fresh water algae.

RE-BACTERIALIZE

The next of the 3 Rs for rebuilding your inner terrain is called *friendly bacteria*. For clarity, friendly bacteria, probiotics, and friendly flora all mean the same thing. They refer to the large array of microorganisms that are naturally found in a healthy intestinal tract, and are absolutely crucial to our well-being. The different types of probiotics in a human gut probably number in the hundreds, but the main ones go by names like *Acidophilus*, *Bifidus*, *Bulgaricus*, and *Salivarius*. These are found in the mouth, throat, stomach, and small and large intestines.

We all have between 4 and 6 pounds of bacteria in our intestinal tract at one time. The key here is not the amount, but the quality. We do not, and cannot remain a sterile environment; if we don't have friendly flora in us, then we have unfriendly flora in us.

Friendly bacteria provide a long list of benefits: they lower cholesterol; create clearer and cleaner skin; control vaginal yeast and inhibit Candida; enhance immunity; and help detoxify harmful substances.

A lack of friendly bacteria has been linked to infections, irritable bowel syndrome, colitis, hemorrhoids, diarrhea, constipation, and chronic malabsorption.

Doing a cleanse reestablishes a gut of friendly bacteria. There are superfoods that are part of the program, such as raw garlic and friendly flora, that help alter your inner terrain so that it is very *unsupportive* of bad bacteria and yeasts (such as Candida), and very *supportive* of the kinds of friendly bacteria that we thrive on.

Similar to a gardener's compost, once an intestinal tract is "seeded", friendly bacteria are capable of reproducing themselves. Yes, they can be destroyed through a variety of modern day insults — chlorinated water, many drugs, fluoride, stress — but it is up to us to replenish, stabilize and support our inner environment for them to thrive and reproduce. We'll show you how to do this in the cleanse.

RE-ENZYMIZE

We introduced the idea of enzymes, the last of the three Rs, and the role they play in both digestion and keeping down the sludge factor, earlier with Digestion Dan's story.

Enzymes are the sparks of life—they run your entire body. You cannot digest or absorb food without them. Your heart will not beat, your lungs won't breathe, and your muscles won't move unless enzymes are present. They are catalysts that, when joined with vitamins and minerals, allow the body to operate.

Most school children have an idea that vitamins and minerals are good for us, but no one is taught that they are useless—literally passed straight through the body—unless they are actively joined by enzymes.

In his book, *Enzyme Nutrition*, Dr. Edward Howell says, *"Our body's life force, vitality, vital force, strength, nerve energy or what ever you choose to call it has enzymes at its core. Without the life energy of enzymes we would be nothing more than a pile of lifeless chemical substances - vitamins, minerals, water and proteins. A body in a weakened, enzyme-deficient state is a prime target for cancer, obesity, heart disease, or other degenerative problems."*

During your cleansing program, there are few things that ease a body through the changes better than enzymes. It is now known that digestive enzymes can actually pass through the intestinal wall and go directly into our bloodstream, where they can break down the metabolic overflow that isn't supposed to be there, substances that the textbooks commonly call *systemic foreign antigens*. Systemic foreign antigens are said to play a major factor in Leaky Gut Syndrome, Fibromyalgia, and Chronic Pain, three of the biggest complaints right now in American and other modern countries. For that reason alone, enzymes belong in the Three Rs, and are part of this cleansing program.

It's not *New and Improved*

It is very important to understand that the Three Rs have always been the foundation of good health. They were the foundation for our grandparents' health, for health in the 1880s, and for health a thousand years ago. Amazon tribes require these same three health fundamentals. In other words, this is not Scott Ohlgren's view of *new and improved*. This is basic human biology.

How, then, did all of those people, past and present, get their Three Rs? And from where?

Minerals were easy; they came from the soil and from the plants and animals the people ate.

Enzymes and friendly bacteria came directly from their foods. The processed *sludge factor foods* were not available. Cheez Swirls and pasteurized milk were not yet the snacks of choice. The enzymes in their food were still intact.

The other sources for enzymes and good bacteria came from (and still comes from) an interesting gastronomic practice common in virtually every long living society: *cultured foods*. These include pickles, yogurt, kefir, umeboshi plums, kimchee, sauerkraut, unheated cheese, sourdough bread, fermented gruels, miso, kombucha tea, and hundreds of others. From Africa to Europe to the Orient, civilizations developed and used fermented, cultured foods.

What do all of these fermented foods have in common? They all contain concentrated, massive amounts of enzymes and friendly bacteria.

We can find foods in the U.S. that appear to be fermented (pickles are one example), but because of our wacky misunderstanding of the microbial world—and our relationship to it—we add one more step to our fermentation process: pasteurization. Pasteurization eliminates virtually all probiotic and enzymatic activity.

All the while we wonder, at the highest levels of education, why we Americans hold the number one position for stomach, colon and other digestive diseases.

Keep learning

We've reached the end of the overall background of Where We Are, and How the heck We Got Here. You now have enough insight into our health situation so that you can successfully experience cellular regeneration in and on your own body.

During the cleanse, I suggest that you keep studying this diet/disease, diet/health connection. For starters, listen to the three CD audobook series, *Real Food, Real Health*. They include *Superfood Secrets, Perfect Skin From Within,* and *The Seven Physical Transformers*. They work well in supporting all of the changes and insights that occur during the program. . They are also highly motivational; to get a sense of that, listen to the free sample sound bites on the How Health Works website.

For information on the entire topic of health, not only the history of why and how we forgot the role of nutrition and ended up believing in chemicals and drugs, as well as a wider view on nutritional cleansing, please check out the Resource Section at the back of this book. You'll find some of the material and authors that I admire and learned from, and books that I wore out over the past two decades. Also view the www.howhealthworks.com site. The more you learn about cellular regeneration, the easier it becomes to get healthy yourself and then pass that knowledge on to others.

On to the NACHO Cleanse.

We live and die at the cellular level. You
can't be healthy if your cells are living
in junk.

Dr. M. Ted Morter

Part Two

The North American Clean the Heck Out 28-Day Cleansing Program

It has been seven weeks since I finished the NACHO Cleanse. I lost 10 pounds during those four weeks, and they haven't reappeared—in fact, I've lost a few more. I'm feeling lighter and healthier than I could have ever anticipated.

However, the most noticeable improvement I've realized is in my emotional state. My mind was clear as a bell after one week, and I was able to notice and handle my emotions much better than I've been able to in a lifetime. I'm a recovered anorexic, and I found that this program gave me the support I needed to finally make a break with my emotional relationship to food. Sugar no longer equals love!! I attribute this to sitting back, watching my food cravings and dealing with them like an adult for the first time.

In fact, I think that in the end, that is what this program does: it teaches us how to eat and relate to food as adults do. That's pretty rare, actually, and I have to say that my self-esteem has soared—if I can nourish myself well without emotional and mental pain (or without stopping because of the pain), what else could I do? The sky's the limit. I'm doing all sorts of things I've always wanted to do, with much less fear and angst. I think the Cleanse helped me cement this new relationship to my life and myself.

Molly Theriault

NACHO Program: The Working Person's Cleanse

The one minute history on the NACHO: The idea of starting a continent-wide cleansing program came out of several conversations between myself and another whole-food teacher, student, and beneficiary of nutritional medicine, Russell Mariani (www.HealthEquest. com). Initially we joked around about doing our annual cleanse at the same time, as a way to compare notes and share some of the funny camaraderie unique to those going through a cleanse ("Hey, how're those bowel movements going?"). But then we thought, wouldn't it be more fun to do this cleanse along with hundreds of others, all scattered across North America? Given our propensity for cheap laughs and irreverence, we searched around for a fun name, and voilà, the **North American Clean the Heck**

Out, aka NACHO, program was born.

The largest motive for opening this cleansing program to others was knowing that most people, both familiar and unfamiliar with a natural foods lifestyle, have actually never done a real cleanse themselves, at least not of this length. There are usually a few reasons for this:

- **They don't know how to do a cleanse.**
- **They don't realize or believe in the benefits that occur during a cleanse.**
- **They don't think they have the necessary will power to complete a cleanse.**
- **They think it requires suffering and hunger.**

If any of these reasons ring true, then this is your chance to get past these blocks. Here is why:

It's easier than you think

The NACHO is a working person's cleanse. It is designed to interrupt your normal life as little as possible. There's not a lot of complexity, you don't starve, and you can choose your own level of commitment and involvement, ranging from beginner to advanced.

NATIONWIDE ONLINE SUPPORT FORUM

You will not be doing your cleansing program alone. An ongoing, on-line forum has been set up specifically for NACHO participants to post their progress reports, questions, concerns, and thoughts to the others who are doing the NACHO program during the same 28-day time slot, all while located in their own homes and kitchens across the continent. This allows for an invaluable conversation of feedback and support.

The significance of this online support feature to past NACHO participants has surprised all of us. By far, it continually has been voted the number one reason that people have pointed to for their success. Why so important? Our guess is because there is strength in numbers. Let's face it, we are creatures of habit. Any time you form a new habit—go to the gym twice a week, stop smoking, quit biting your nails, even something as simple as change eating choices—you feel better if you know that there are others doing that change, or who have done that change, along with you. You'll see this clearly by going online and reading the amazing and oftentimes moving stories (www. howhealthworks.com/forum).

These posts from past and current participants can give you a surprising emotional and psychological strength that keep you committed, and keep you going. You start to see that what you are going through is not unique, and that others are there to cheer you on. It is all part of the goal to make this cleansing adventure not only effective, educational, and motivational, but also the start of a movement that changes the public's perception of where our symptoms and illness really come from.

What exactly is Cellular Cleansing?

Cellular cleansing is a method of using certain nutrition and lifestyle guidelines that have been found to be effective for flushing the body of built-up toxins that accumulate over time from a variety of sources, and thus return the body to a higher level of health. This is done through a twofold process:

First, we intentionally minimize or eliminate certain foods, habits and influences for a designated period of time—in our case, 28 days.

Second, we intentionally bring in the foods, habits and techniques that are well-known to help cleanse, nourish and regenerate the body. Our miraculous body does the rest.

In our experience, nothing comes close to the potential for profound health changes like a cellular cleanse. **Nothing.** In fact, many people report that even after years and years of "eating well" they did not really have a jump in health, or the removal of longtime symptoms, until they took the time, and created the willpower, to do a purposeful cellular cleansing and detoxification program. If you are more than 10 years old, and have never done a cellular cleanse, then you do not know how healthy you can be.

This program is not a "fast." You will not go hungry during this cleanse. This is a cellular *flush,* not a fast. Being hungry is not the objective. As a matter of fact, it's against the rules to go hungry during the NACHO (we've had to jail a few participants who didn't eat enough). Instead, your job is to do the steps that flush the cells of their accumulated toxicity, and replace them with a higher level of nutrition and vitality.

If you have heard horror stories from others who have done cleansing programs, rest assured. This cleanse is specifically designed to be effective, but also easy for the average hard-working Joe/Josephine.

Who should do a cleanse

The honest and straightforward answer: EVERYONE.
Which cars should get an oil change?

Think of a cleansing program as the body's oil change. Then realize that most North Americans have never, ever changed their internal oil.

In a cleaner, more toxin-free body, you can experience more health benefits than ever before. If you are seriously committed to optimum health, periodic cleansing is not optional; it is mandatory.

Preparation is the key

There are 5 overall guidelines that we have seen make for a successful and life motivating cleanse:

1. Choose a definitive start and stop date.

2. Choose a cleansing level that best fits your situation.

3. Organize yourself and your kitchen.

4. Commit to breaking through insulting habits.

5. Learn about cellular detoxification.

Let's dig further into these five guidelines in this next section.

The Five Preparation Guidelines

If you woke up this morning, thinking, "Wow, I gotta get back into shape... hmm, I know! I'll run a marathon!", it would be not be advisable to go to your closet, put on your sneakers, and then jog 26.2 miles later that afternoon. Some preparation and pre-conditioning might be a good idea.

Same goes for the NACHO cleanse. **You cannot do this program without some forethought and planning. It won't work.** We're simply too habituated in our routines, and this cleanse will challenge those routines, and that takes planning.

This section will give you the steps necessary for breaking through those routines and allow for a successful, stress-free NACHO.

#1. Choose a definitive start and stop date.

Start your NACHO cleanse on the first of the month. You decide which month that will be, but start it on the first, and end it on the 28th, so that your own program coincides with the online portion of the NACHO. Knowing exactly when you are starting, and exactly when you are stopping, will give you a psychological advantage as well. There is power in knowing that this challenge runs for exactly *these* 28 days, and on the 29th day, you can go back to eating anything and everything you want (as you'll see in the chapter titled What Next? *After The Nacho,* this is one of the post-cleanse strategies. Sort of like the "so you want to smoke, do you? Okay, smoke the whole pack right here, son" strategy some of us were introduced to as kids).

Take a look at the following preparation guidelines, as well as your own work and life schedule. Then decide the month you will go for it.

Once you've chosen your month, go to www.howhealthworks.com and sign up for the NACHO. It's free, you can remain anonymous, and you'll start receiving some free goodies and specials. You'll also get access to posting on the NACHO bulletin board. Be sure you sign up at *least* seven days before the first of the month. This will give you time to do the necessary preparation. You'll then receive the Welcome Newsletter, which includes your refrigerator calendar. Print a copy, fill out the dates, and place it on your refrigerator. This will become the focal point for keeping you on track.

#2. Choose a cleansing level

Read through the next chapter, *The NACHO Cleanse.* Look over the requirements for the basic bare-bones cleanse, as well as the more advanced elements that you can add in. Read from the online bulletin board for the results that past participants have received.

Then answer some questions: Is this your first cleanse? Have you ever eliminated a food from your diet before? How busy is your day? Do you have easy access to your kitchen, the organic foods, your juicer, etc. Are you doing this alone or with some buddies? What results are you looking for? Do you have a life-debilitating or life-threatening set of symptoms? Do you feel fairly toxic these days or are you looking just for a basic tune up?

All of these questions and thoughts will give you a better feel for the level of cleanse that is best suited for you and your current life situation. As you'll see, there are different levels of participation, from the basic model to more advanced cleanses. It's important to note that they all lie on the same continuum, each building from the same baseline **5 Musts**. From easy to more difficult. From a walk in the park, I-hardly-can-tell-I'm-on-a-cleanse, to fairly intense.

We'll go into more detail later on, but here are the 5 Musts of the **Basic NACHO Cleanse:**

1. REMOVE MUCUS FORMING FOODS: To your best ability, make it a mucusless 28 days. Mucus makers include dairy, ice cream, eggs, flour, hydrogenated oil, baked flour products and highly processed foods.

2. DAILY JUICING: Daily consumption of around 32 ounces of fresh juice from raw fruits and vegetables (no frozen or pasteurized).

3. INCREASE THE *THREE Rs*: As you recall, these are the replacements for the 3 missing elements in a modern day diet: ReMineralize, ReBacterialize, and ReEnzymize. These also happen to be the common denominator of most cleansing programs: increase of mineral-rich foods, increase of enzymes and enzyme rich foods, and the rebacterialization of the large and small intestines. This will happen naturally through your cleansing dietary change, but we will also be using supplementation to multiply the results.

4. REMOVE REFINED SUGAR FOODS: (candies, cakes, cookies, muffins, ice cream, soda, etc.). If you have never gone a month without white sugar, then you have no idea of its ill effects on your health, your skin, your emotions, and your thinking abilities. It's time for a break.

5. REHYDRATE YOUR CELLS: Each day, you'll be drinking a minimum of half your body weight in ounces of pure spring water.

These 5 Musts are what comprise the Basic NACHO cleanse. Write these down. Print them up. Put them on your refrigerator, your computer screen, and your bathroom mirror. If you do NOTHING ELSE during these 28 days— just four short weeks— but the above five suggestions, you will succeed in your cleanse and get great results and changes.

Your main objective is to FINISH the 28 days. Going "cold turkey, 100% all out" isn't always possible, and not even necessary. Setting a goal for cutting back to 30, 40, or 60 percent of your normal foods may be what works for you, your lifestyle, and your temperament. Taper down your craving foods in the weeks leading up to your NACHO cleanse. Don't set up your cleanse so it's too difficult to win. Remember, you are winning just by participating in the program.

#3. Organize yourself and your kitchen

Don't wait until the morning of the first day to start. It simply will not work. Prepare yourself—and your kitchen —in advance.

MAKE A CLEANSING KITCHEN

Look through your kitchen and pantry. Be sure that the only ingredients in your kitchen are those supportive of your cleanse. Now would be good time to throw out those surplus M&Ms, half cartons of ice cream, the cookies, spare crackers, the partial bag of white sugar, canned foods, pasteurized milk and juices, the hidden stash of Debbie Cakes®, and anything that contains ingredients you can't pronounce. If you have never participated in the "cleansing and detoxification" of your refrigerator, pantry, and kitchen cupboards, this is a great time to have that experience. Get it all out of your house. Give it to an unsuspecting friend, or neighbor with whom you don't get along. Remember, you can always restock those Debbie Cakes, if you so desire.

I've seen people break into a nervous sweat during this first step. Throwing out that hidden chocolate cache can bring up something akin to primal fear. People will often look like they're going to die just thinking about it. **Remember, you will not go hungry during this program.** As a matter of fact, hunger is forbidden. You are simply going to replace your normal caloric choices with cleansing ones. Take a breath, whimper all you want, then toss or give it away.

JUICERS

If you don't have a juicer, it is time to either borrow one from a friend, or buy one that will last you the rest of your life. **Your juicer will now be the focal point of your kitchen for these 28 days.** Put it out on the counter, and **do not put it away for the duration.** Let it replace your toaster oven and microwave.

Suggested Juicers

It used to be that the only real heavy-duty juicer out there was a 40-year-old American-built workhorse called the Champion. This juicer was instrumental in helping America understand the power of fresh juice. My family had one for years, but as an ex-carpenter and builder, I always knew there could be a better design waiting to be made.

Fortunately, juicers have gone through a revolution in design in just the past few years. Much safer, slower speeds for less oxidation, and fast cleanup.

There are now over 50 juicers available on the market. They range from underpowered $80 units created by engineers who could not have ever made a glass of carrot juice in their lives, to the exorbitantly priced $2,000 behemoths of stainless steel overkill and silliness.

In the search for the best juicers, and after a lot of hands-on testing, I've found one innovative model that stands head and shoulders above the rest: the **twin-helical gear juicer.** From an engineering standpoint, it is a revolutionary twist on the question of how you squeeze

juice out of a turnip (and other vegetables). If you currently own a juicer, and then see this twin gear unit in action, you realize that its designers were thinking outside of any for-mer juicer design constraints. This helps explain why the twin-helical design has won international design awards since its original inception in the early nineties.

We became so enamored with the innovation of the twin gear juicer that we contacted its manufacturer and now carry it on the How Health Works website.

That said, **any juicer will work,** and help you attain better health. If you have one, use it. If you're in the market for a new one, here are some guidelines:

Multi-purpose. Get a juicer that handles both **vegetables** *and* **wheatgrass** effectively (in the past, you needed a separate unit for making wheatgrass), as well as nuts, leafy greens, ginger, and other highly fibrous foods.

Hard to clog up. Easy and fast cleanup. With the pace of modern life, we need a juicer that doesn't require cleaning every 5 minutes, and can deal with heavy loads, and can clean up in a couple of minutes.

Long warranties. Three to five year warranties are now normal. Get a juicer that could withstand small nuclear bombs, and will outlive all of us (even those who periodically do cleansing).

Quiet operation. Well-balanced motors.

Very effective juicing. Leaves the pulp dry.

Powerful motors, slow RPMs. Turn at safer 160-180 revolutions (versus some that spin between 1,200 and 6,000 revolutions per minute).

Longer lasting juice. Low RPM heat means no oxidation, and a healthier juice. The juice actually lasts longer, since there is less oxidation occurring.

Safe. Some juicers have no safety switch. Look for a juicer that makes it hard to hurt yourself.

GET YOUR SUPPLIES AND SOURCES READY

Use the following as a check off list:

Vegetable and fruit juicing requirements. Purchase 25 pound bags of both carrots and beets. Get a case of apples (or 4 gallons of raw, *unpasteurized* apple juice), 10 pounds of lemons, 3 pounds each of garlic and ginger root. You'll be juicing all of these with their skins on, so finding organic sources is important. Even the smallest health food stores can special order these items, if given enough lead time.

Fresh trays of wheatgrass. If there's not a local source that will juice it for you, or sell you whole trays, be prepared to grow your own. It's easy, and made even easier by companies such as *WheatGrassKits.com*. Their kits are inexpensive and contain everything you need. Take it from a complete gardening idiot who can kill a potted plant from 10 paces away out of sheer fright, nothing is easier than growing your own wheat grass.

Organic superfood supplements. Since wild-crafted algae, both ocean and fresh water, are one of the easier ways to remineralize our tissues, I have advocated and daily consumed algae for years.

Here is a suggested list:

    1 bottle of probiotics
    1 jar of freeze dried supergreen drink
    1 bottle of blue green algae
    1 herbal colon cleanse
    2 bottles of enzymes (the best you can find)

Celtic Gray Sea Salt. The best and most direct source is through *The Grain & Salt Society*. Your local health food store may carry their imported salt, but it's often difficult to find true Celtic Gray salt still in crystal form. Get a pound for the best price. Their website is www.celtic-sea-salt.com, and their phone is 1 800-TOP SALT.

Hydration jug. This is nothing more than the one container that you will fill up each morning with your H_2O requirements, and be sure it's empty by the time you go to bed. This eliminates guesswork, and helps remind you of the cleanse throughout each day. This can be a plastic, one gallon jug that many liquids come in, or one you buy in the store. No matter, just have it on hand, and use it.

The first 3 tapes in the *3-CD audiobook, Real Food, Real Health: How to eat our way back to a health nation: Superfood Secrets, Perfect Skin from Within,* and *The Seven Physical Transformers*. These explain the key pieces about cleansing, they are motivational and purposefully inexpensive for NACHO participants. Listen to them in the car to help reinforce what you're learning.

Body Therapists. There are two types of body work recommended during a cleanse: deep physical manipulation, and colon hydrotherapy. If you don't already know these types of practitioners, ask around for local referrals and check the Resources section of the HHW site. Then, schedule in your sessions well in advance. For more specifics on the kinds of work recommended during your cleanse, see **The Seven Physical Transformers** chapter.

Keep a daily journal. Set aside 5-15 minutes each day to record your questions, insights, and observations. Given the changes that are possible, you will want to keep a permanent record of this experience.

MENTALLY, SOCIALLY AND PSYCHOLOGICALLY PREPARE

Set up the game so you win.

Take a good look at your program calendar (again, a full size version one can be downloaded from the HHW site), and study it. Look at the dates: you start *here,* and you end *on this date.* This will let your brain start thinking, "I can do this." Put one of the calendars on your refrigerator. Be ready to mark off the days as they are completed. Think of the celebration you will have after the last day of the cleanse. Most people have NEVER given their body a rest from sugar, for instance. This is a true achievement. Prepare for that celebration now.

Don't underestimate the role of a positive, YES attitude. Your goal is to finish the 28 days. Keep it fun. Plan to laugh at yourself at least once a day. Twice for some of you (and you know who you are).

It's worth mentioning again, going "cold turkey, 100% all out" isn't always possible, nor is it necessary. Set a goal for simply cutting back on your normal intake on your regular foods. Don't set up your cleanse so it's too difficult to win.

Think ahead, you do not want to be in a situation where your friends bring a nice tin of cookies and vanilla ice cream over to the house to share during your cleanse. You may want to alert your associates and family about what you are doing, and invite their cooperation…and possibly their participation.

Purchase or download your reading and audio material, and start studying now. Education can be the best medicine by itself.

Be prepared to set out your daily food, juice and supplement program the night before or first thing in the morning, so you can track your consumption. This will avoid the "whoops I forgot!" days, and help you keep to your regimen.

Never be hungry. Nothing will destroy your incentive and willpower more than hunger. So don't put yourself in the position to get hungry. Since most of the normal means of feeding yourself aren't an option during a cleanse, you'll need to think ahead: when you're traveling in your car, do you have cleansing snack foods, fresh juice, and water? Is there a juice bar along the way where you can replenish and refresh? Again, this is *not* a fast. Those have their place, but this isn't one of them. Think of this more as the working man/working woman's cleansing program, where you have enough calories and full stomach feeling to keep going with your life.

#4 Commit to
overcoming insulting habits

We all consume certain items that, when removed from our diet, elicit a feeling closely resembling *withdrawal*. As you will soon find out, street drugs are definitely not the only substances that create a craving when we eliminate them from our daily habits. Prevailing through these initial cravings and habitual food addictions is one of the side benefits of the NACHO.

There are few health-related things more exhilarating than giving your body a break from a bad habit. For example, most of us have never gone 28 days without white sugar. NOTE: if you accomplish only this one goal during your cleanse, you will probably experience the largest increase in your health—and removal of long standing symptoms— you have ever seen. The same goes for what is termed "fake fat"; if you were born after 1945, chances are very good that your body has never been 28 days free of the ravages of hydrogenated fat.

There are some powerful tricks you can use to avoid the 'bonk' of your hardest addictions. The biggest trick is, believe it or not, water. Because of sugar's ability of pulling water from cells, the saying goes, *"If you are craving sugar, it means you are dehydrated. Always!"* If you suddenly start *jonesing* (craving strongly) for a Snickers® bar, immediately drink a quart of water. Not a cup—a quart. Always rehydrate this way before making any rash decisions and bending to your habitual responses. Other tips: If you're working during the day, and don't have time for meal prep, prepare a quart of lemonade, made with fresh squeezed lemons, a pinch of Celtic sea salt, and a bit of dark maple syrup (the darker and "lower" the grade, the more minerals left in the syrup). Drink fresh juices every 1-2 hours. The simple sugars in them will help you transition out of the White Sugar Blues. There will be other tips throughout this manual.

Use only olive, hemp, and flax oil during the NACHO. Use enough to prevent the **grease and fat cravings**.

If you're getting off caffeinated drinks, taper down the weeks before actually starting the cleanse. Check your local health food store for specialized homeopathic formulas designed for just such a purpose. Same goes for smoking. They'll have names such as "Caffeinease", "Smokease", etc.

It is normal to feel the pull of habitual responses during a cleanse. But as thousands of people who have gone before you can explain, it can be life changing to break the chains of insulting habits and addictions. Because of the volume of nutrient dense fuel that you will be feeding yourself, you may find it easier to deal with than ever before. Just one more advantage to this cleansing process.

RESETTING THE DEFAULT BUTTON
ON YOUR TASTE BUDS

The *single largest topic* of emails I receive from NACHO participants is about cravings. When you're jonesing/craving for chocolate cake and milk, you'll start to understand why. So let's tackle this topic before moving on.

First, some craving-related history: In 1984, I attended a nine month, three semester school called the Kushi Institute, in Brookline, Massachusetts. The school explored the relationship between food and disease/health, and that exploration naturally started with each student's own dietary changes. Although most of my 30 classmates were already eating a different food chain than the one they had grown up with, it was still a shock to jump into a diet that eliminated all dairy, all white sugar, and all heavily processed foods. Each of us learned an enormous amount about cravings during that first month or so. What drives them, where they come from, how to change them, and what they really are.

The first thing we learned about cravings was that they were so obviously connected to our taste buds— meaning, we all eat what our taste buds have become used to. Daily, they tell us what is delicious. We also learned that most of us just assumed that our taste buds were IN CONTROL, they were set in stone, since birth, and there was nothing we could do about that. "I have a sweet tooth." "I don't like vegetables." "I really like fatty foods." We didn't think these phrases were choices; we thought of them as our destiny.

The second thing we learned: **taste buds can be radically altered**. One of the first times I realized this was about six weeks into the program during a dinner at the study house where I lived with 12 other students. We were all sitting down to our normal seven-course meal we had prepared, and one of the plates being served was *nashime*, a very slowly cooked root vegetable dish, that contains nothing but a piece of kombu seaweed, large two inch chunks of a variety of root vegetable, a half inch of water, and sea salt. After my first bite of some off-white root I didn't recognize, I thought, "They used sugar! There's no way a vegetable could be this sweet! Awwright!" When I asked the cooks, though, they said, no, there wasn't any sugar added, and I was just tasting the natural sweetness coming out of the parsnip. After five weeks off of all processed sugar, my mouth was finding sweetness in root veggies.

Another example was with dairy foods. First, you have to realize I was born and raised in Wisconsin, where the phrase "the dairy state" is plastered proudly on every license plate, and where I am fairly certain that it is illegal to consume less than a gallon of milk per week. I loved cheese. I had lived on cheese while traveling through Europe, Africa, and Australia in my twenties. How was I ever going to stop eating and liking Camembert? But I did; I left my last slice of Provolone on the first day of school, and didn't touch dairy foods for the entire duration.

Shortly after graduation, though, I visited a friend who was holding a large potluck dinner. Many of the dishes were, as normal, based in milk and cheese products. Being in a *"party down, dude"* attitude that evening, I decided to loosen up and try out the cream of asparagus soup. To this day, I can still remember the revulsion of smelling and tasting that soup. The phrase "coagulated cow mucus" will forever stick in my mind.

I'm not telling these stories to say that Satan Lives in Dairy Products, and that you can't ever party down... dude. I'm telling the story to point out that **your taste buds aren't permanent. Your cravings are only habit.** You can *reset the default button on your mouth* within a month or two of eating fewer processed foods. And you don't know what health really is until you are free from habits.

One of the things you will notice after your NACHO cleanse is that you will not be able to sit down and eat the same things, in the same amounts, that you did before. Eating as much sugar as you used to will make you sick. Just staring at the fat lying on the top of that pizza you once consume twice a week will turn your stomach. Smelling that glass of milk will make you wonder why you'd never noticed the "coagulated cow mucus" smell before. Why? Because you've given your taste buds a chance to find their neutral gear. You've reset the default switch. Your organs no longer require those extremes to be satisfied.

BREAKING THROUGH THE INSULTING HABITS

So until cooked parsnips and an apple satisfy your sugar craving, and olive oil works for your oil and fat needs, be sure to STAY HYDRATED. You will be amazed at the difference in your sugar cravings, and it's why we recommend Dr. Batmanghelidj and his www.watercure.com site and books. Have fruit around. Be sure you're consuming enough fresh veggie juices. They're filled with simple sugars. Put seeds and nuts in your morning whole grain cooked cereals. Use nuts and olive oil in your salads. Cook with enough oil in your meals so you don't crave greasy foods and cheeses. And check out www.notmilk.com to learn more about the damaging effects that pasteurized dairy food is having on our health.

#5 Learn about cellular detoxification

This last NACHO rule, what could be called "cleansing education," is an extremely critical piece to a successful 28 days, yet is the one most overlooked. Mentioned earlier, this cannot be said enough: **Misinterpreting the changes that occur when you replace your regular food for cleansing food, is, bar none, the most common mistake made, and why some will not complete the cleanse.** This will start to make more sense once you fully appreciate the powerful hold our current health paradigm has on our thinking. Educating yourself to get beyond the "chasing symptoms" approach will be a key factor in your success.

UNDERSTANDING DETOXIFICATION

One of the hardest parts about improving and changing your nutritional intake is that your body will often use that change as an opportunity to flush out its 100 trillion cells. This phenomenon is called a *cleansing reaction*, or *detoxification.*

Have you ever known someone who stopped smoking? Chances are they will tell you stories of coughing fits, expelling foul mucus from the lungs, aches and pains in their muscles, black circles appearing under their eyes, all sorts of symptoms that show up in those first few weeks after quitting.

Ever know anyone who stopped drinking coffee? They will tell you stories of pounding headaches, joint pain, feeling like their kidneys were going to fall out of their back, constipation, extreme fatigue, dehydration, etc.

What is happening to these people? If stopping these things is supposed to be so good for you, why are they having these symptoms that appear once they stop the assumed toxin?

It's called cleansing. Their body is cleaning itself out. Given the first opportunity to incorporate and remake itself with higher-quality nutrients, a body will dump the old material into any channel that it has available—the blood, the lymph system, the tissues, the excretory organs, the skin, the lungs— in order to make room for the new. This process is the heart of all regeneration. It is why you and I can heal, and why we can improve our health.

This cellular regeneration is happening in our bodies all the time, whether you're doing a NACHO-type cleanse or not. We have been "cleansing" from the moment of conception all the way to this minute right here, right now. Most of the time, though, this exchanging of "old for new" isn't noticed, or more accurately, it's noticed only through what we view as the normal channels of cleansing (over 30% of the every bowel movement is in fact dead cells). This all happens at a rate that is comfortable, and through normal metabolic processes, because you're using the same fuel that you've used for years. Change that fuel, though, to a much cleaner, more nutrient-dense fuel— like the fuel you'll be feeding yourself during the NACHO—and you may well feel and see this "sped-up metabolism" taking place.

THE SYMPTOM LIST

There are many, many ways detoxification will show up in and on your body when metabolic waste starts leaving the cells. The unfortunate crime is that every single one of these symptoms are normally translated in our culture as **"Wow, I am getting sick, I am getting worse, and I need drugs to stop this symptom from occurring."** The list is long, but here are a few signs to be aware of:

Headaches
Colds/Flu symptoms
Fever/ Chills
Joint pains
Coughing
Gas and Bloating
Fatigue
Hives
Increased menstruation

Decreased menstruation
Cramps
Rashes
Bad Breath
Dandruff
Excess ear wax
Excess nose gunk
Excess throat sludge
Constipation
Diarrhea
Wheezing
Tight/stiff neck
Acne
Backaches
Itchy skin
Red skin
Sleep interruption
Dizziness
Mood changes
Irritation

You get the idea. Instead of memorizing the list, the key is to realize that we experience these symptoms as a result of our body burning off metabolic waste. **This is a good thing.** The alternative is to keep that waste in us, in our cells. Once you complete a cleansing program, you will start to detect, visually, how a majority of people walk around with their cells filled with this old, necrotic material; the connections between a diseased state and that necrotic overflow will become more and more apparent. For now, though, it's just important that you view this detoxification process as the road to a higher level of health.

How to ease through detox

Fortunately, there are several powerful methods built into the NACHO cleanse that ease the body through nutritional cleansing.

The first is water. Lots of it. Imagine, for a moment, a clean flowing stream running through your front yard of your mountain cabin. One day your neighbors upstream decide to do a yard "cleanse" and dumps huge amounts of dirt, old leaves, and debris into the stream. Within a short period of time, your clean water has become clogged with debris, and starts running very slowly. The best way get things cleared up is to first *slow down the Toxic Load*, by having the neighbor stop putting that much waste into the stream at one time. The other, though, is by increasing the water flow. This holds true in your body as well. If you know ahead of time that a large majority of your 100 trillion cells are all about to dump their old ingredients into your "river," it behooves you to radically increase the amount of water and liquids that we are drinking, to keep the flow going.

The second method of easing cleansing symptoms is enzymes. Encapsulated enzymes are one of the most powerful ways of speeding up metabolic detox I have ever seen. This makes sense: digestive enzymes are now known to be able to pass *through the intestinal wall* and go directly into our bloodstream and tissues, where they can break down undigested proteins, and other matter, commonly referred to as *systemic foreign antigens*. Let's speak frankly here, what do you think a "systemic foreign antigen" is? It's not a whole lot different from the material that we refer to as our bowel movement. In other words, our poop is leaking into the tissues of our body. Knowing that makes it easier to understand the role this stuff plays in Leaky

Gut Syndrome, Fibromyalgia, and Chronic Pain, three oftentimes-related symptoms that are currently among the biggest health complaints in the United States. For this reason alone, encapsulated enzymes are part of the NACHO superfood supplements.

Another way to ease metabolic detox is through the use of foods high in chlorophyll, a well-known blood purifier. We'll do this through daily consumption of **leafy greens, wild blue green algae,** and **wheatgrass.**

The most obvious way of easing any of the above cleansing symptoms is simply regulating the speed of your program. For example, slowly tapering down your normal coffee intake, or pint-a-day ice cream fix, instead of going cold turkey. Conversely, you can also adjust the superfoods that you're using. If you're up to 4 shots of wheat grass and 6 caps of algae per day, and you are getting overrun with cleansing symptoms, it is time to cut these potent cleansers in half for a few days, to give your body's "river" time to clean up what has landed there.

The last group of tricks for both easing up, and speeding up, the detoxification process is through what I call the *Seven Physical Transformers.* These are such a powerful set of tools that there is a whole chapter on them later in the book.

DON'T GET FOOLED BY LOOKS

All of these tips help us get a new, more accurate perception on the discharging and detoxification that occurs during a cleanse. Bar none, the most misunderstood aspect of healing and health is the way we interpret our symptoms. Remember, we are the culture that thinks dandruff has something to do with the scalp and a bad hair day, instead of realizing that it's the overflow of a liver filled with hard fat and protein excess; we think a stuffed-up nose comes from some bug, instead of realizing the role that our mucus-laden white flour and hydrogenated fat sugar-cookie diet has played in its creation.

In the twenty years I have been involved in nutrition, not a week has gone by without some version of the following scenario being played out:

A person starts a nutritional cleansing program. The cleanse works well, immediately pushing out large amounts of life-deadening, disease producing, symptom creating internal gunk, formed over the years by this person's lifestyle and meal choices. This internal gunk comes out through their nose, their throat, their lungs, their ears, their liver, their skin, their colon, their breath and their throat, helping to create the symptoms that most people know as "A Cold", or "The Flu". Upon seeing all this, the cleansing participant slips into automatic behavior, stops by the pharmacy on the way home, and picks up a variety of drugs that are designed for one thing: **stopping the internal gunk from coming out.** For clarity, let's just call all of these drugs the StoppingTheInternalGunkFromComingOut drugs.

I've seen people break out in a rash during a cleanse— fine, call it acne, hives, underarm rash, pimples on their back, itchiness, eczema, psoriasis, red chest inflammation, Rosacea, WHATEVER. They freak out and go to a dermatologist who dutifully applies one of the Stopping-The-Internal-Gunk-From-Coming-Out drugs, such as cortisone cream, Accutane, etc., to stop the rash from appearing, whereas the person thereby feels better because the rash or other breakout is now gone. Accutane and cortisone cream are, of course, both well-known *liver toxins*.

The person then continues on a cleansing diet, and the body uses the cleansing foods to expel the drugs now stored in the fat cells of the liver, which are pushed out again through the skin and hair, creating more visible signs and symptoms, which of course further freaks out this cleansing program person, who goes back for a second dermatologist visit, and says, "The Stopping-The-Internal-Gunk-From-Coming-Out drugs you gave me aren't strong enough. Got anything better?".

The skin doctor, being a good person who wants to diminish suffering, prescribes a stronger more toxic Stopping-The-Internal-Gunk-From-Coming-Out drug, which then also has to leave the body through the skin, until finally the person gives up the cleansing program because *that really strange juicing program that I was doing was making me sick.*

I've seen many, many people, upon learning that this is what may come out of their body during a switch to cleansing foods, *stop the cleanse, and choose to keep that metabolic sludge in them.* And we wonder why our country's rise in diseases seems to "appear out of nowhere." Why little Johnnie can't concentrate in school. Why childhood diabetes is almost *20 times* what it was in 1960.

Fuel your determination with knowledge. A new perception of how health really works, and why the body is doing what it is doing, is needed all the more so during a cleanse. Read everything you can on cleansing, not only other books on the art of cleansing, but especially other people's end results and testimonials. **You need to hear from those who have completed a cleanse, who can tell you what it feels like on the other side.** You need to realize the powerful actions that you are taking during these four weeks on the NACHO, and the results that are happening at a cellular level. Listen to the audio and video materials. Talk with others who are also going through this process.

I was shocked to see what my normal food intake was doing to my body. This program gave me improved sleep, fewer mood swings and I just felt better. The best result of the cleanse, though, was the general pleasure that I experienced from breaking my regular eating and drinking habits. My taste buds seemed to open up. As some-one who loves to cook and eat, I found this to be one of the largest benefits.

As far as the old food habits, I'm glad to be rid of them. Thanks for organizing this effort.

Ezra Simon-Gollogly

What to Expect From Your Cleanse

No one finishes a cleanse unaltered. I have yet to see a person experience zero improvements. How much improvement, and what exactly improves, will vary widely, from mild to life changing and life saving. It depends on a large variety of factors, including body types, present conditions, mental beliefs, cleansing foods used, and more. What is more important to focus on is this: you are about to enter a 28-day period that can change your life.

In general, here are the most common benefits and improvements following a cleansing program:

- Increased energy and vitality
- Reduction of stress and anxiety
- Reduction of mood swings
- Improved Immunity
- Proper weight maintenance

- Lessening of present disease/illness symptoms
- Increase joint flexibility
- Decrease joint pain/inflammation
- Improved memory, mental clarity and concentration
- Improved skin, hair and nails
- Overall feeling of well-being
- Eradicating depression
- Increased physical stamina
- Fewer colds and flu symptoms
- Renewed sense of purpose in life

Seven Percent

One of the real crimes about cleansing and the overall "getting healthier" movement is that so many people have it mentally wired that the only way to cleanse or get healthy is to "do it the right way." To these people, this means "Doing it 100 percent or not doing it at all!"

I have dear friends, as close to my heart as can be, who for ten or twenty years have struggled in the throes of bad nutritional and lifestyle habits. Every year, they continue to add more body weight, more "Chronic Fatigue," more physical pain, more names to their growing list of symptoms, more metabolic waste build-up. They have become a walking time bomb of toxic load in deep need of cellular cleansing.

Once or twice each year, these friends get a spurt of determination to clean up their internal terrain. They buy the juicer, order some superfoods, throw away the candy bars and white bread, get a new pair of running shoes, and then wake up in the morning ready to go "one hundred and ten percent!".

Within three days, they're back to square one and their old lifestyle.

Why? Because they have no concept of **gradation** and **gradual conditioning**. They think the "all or nothing" is the only approach, and never see the guilt trip that sneaks up on them and bites them in the butt.

To those who have found themselves stuck in the "I'm not doing it right" "I can't stay committed" "See, I cheat all the time, I knew I was a loser" scenarios, I have one thing to say: give me seven percent change. Seven percent less ice cream consumption. Seven percent less sugar; seven percent more fresh juice every day; seven percent more of the Three Rs. Seven percent more deep breathing. That's it. Do as much as you can, but most people do not need a radical change to start experiencing better cell regeneration.

Why seven percent? It's small enough to slip under the mental, physical, and psychological radar that has prevented you from seeing the real, spiritual you, and yet still get results. It's small enough so that it won't kick up any cravings, won't give you any sense of deprivation, and won't even be noticed. With the Seven Percent Solution, all you need to succeed is your word. If you have the resolve to stick to your word, for just 28 days, then you can complete this cleanse.

No Excuses

Nutritional cleansing has a very long history; it's mentioned in the Bible and other religious texts. Hippocrates was a fan. Kellogg (of cereal fame) and numerous health writers of this century all promoted periodic cleansing. Although there are many, many correlations and similarities to these cleansing programs going back thousands of years, there are a few places where there are differences of opinion:

- Salt, or no salt?
- All raw, or some cooked?
- Mountain spring water, or distilled?
- Fruit, or no fruit?
- Supplementation, or only things that grow directly from the ground?
- Colon therapy, or let the colon do its own thing?
- 100% plant-based diet, or some animal products?

Here is the NACHO's radical variance of opinion:

Experiment. See for yourself. Try different approaches. Don't take any particular method too seriously.

There are also certain specific companies and products that are recommended to use throughout and after your NACHO cleanse. Examples include a sea salt produced in France, a line of organic supplements and wild algae from an Oregon-based company, two particular Maine and California ocean-harvested sea vegetable farmers, certain books, authors, ideas, websites hosted by both medical doctors as well as lay people, and a few other suggestions.

If you like some other kind of enzyme supplement, and

don't like the one suggested in this book, don't let that stop you from doing a cleanse. If you don't want to use Celtic Gray sea salt, you don't have to. Don't let it stop you from doing a cleanse. If you think the NACHO name is silly, or you don't like me or something I said or suggested in this book, don't let it stop you from doing a cleanse. If drinking distilled water sounds better than drinking mountain spring water, do that. If you'd prefer to use only raw foods, and forego all cooked foods, do that instead. If you don't have the money to use supplements, or don't like supplements period, or are a weight lifter and no way in hell are you going stop eating meat twice a day, or can't afford a great juicer, or can't stand the taste of wheat grass... whatever the reason, **do not let it stop you from doing a cellular cleanse.**

There is no excuse for not experiencing cellular cleansing. NONE.

Every suggestion mentioned here is because of my own good results. I've used most of them for well over 12 years. I've traveled to Klamath Lake to see wild algae being harvested. I personally knew the founder of the Celtic sea salt company, Jacques de Langre. I've spoken to the farmers who carefully and diligently harvest their ocean sea vegetables, and have used their sea vegetables for almost two decades. I've done the saunas, hundreds of shiatsu massages, and have utilized colonics for years and years. I suggest them because I've seen them work.

But they're still just suggestions. You can do this cleanse in a way that works for you.

Ready? Let's do the NACHO.

This was the first cleanse I have ever done. I saw changes immediately. The chronic constipation was gone, as was the constant heartburn. I had many days I could actually say "I feel good today."

Once I got into the routine, this cleanse was like clock work for me, very easy to follow and be consistent with.

Debra Burcar

The NACHO Cleanse

This chapter explains The 28-day NACHO Cleansing Program.

For the next 28 days, you will begin the process of rebuilding your blood, your tissues, your organs, your Immunity, all from the ground up.

Here again are the preparation steps:

Choose a definitive start and stop date. Go online, and sign up for the NACHO, and download the calendar. You'll be starting on the first of the month.

Choose a cleansing level that best fits your situation.

Organize yourself and your kitchen. Get your supplies ready.

Commit to breaking through insulting habits.

Commit to learning about cellular detoxification.

Here again are the 4 Steps to Cleansing:

1. Slowing down the Toxic Load
2. Remineralizing
3. ReBacterializing
4. ReEnzymizing

Here again are the 5 Basics of the NACHO:

REMOVE MUCUS-FORMING FOODS: To your best ability, make it a mucusless 28 days. These include: dairy, ice cream, eggs, flour products, and highly processed oils and foods.

DAILY JUICING: Daily consumption of about 32 ounces of fresh juice from raw fruits and vegetables.

INCREASE THE THREE Rs: Gradually increase the 3 most essential ingredients to our modern day food chain: ReMineralize, ReBacterialize, ReEnzymize.

REMOVE REFINED SUGAR FOODS: If you've never gone a month without white sugar, you have no idea of its ill effects on your health, your skin, your emotions, your thinking abilities, etc.

REHYDRATE YOUR CELLS: Each day, drink half your body weight in ounces of pure spring water.

Write these down. Print them up. Put them on your refrigerator, your computer screen, your bathroom mirror. If you do NOTHING ELSE during these 28 days— just 4 short weeks—you will succeed in your cleanse and get great results and changes. Your overall goal is to KEEP IT SIMPLE by focusing on only these five things.

98

The daily To-Do's

Here is the list of things to do and consume each day:

- **Juice about 32 ounces of fresh juice each day** (obviously, if you only weigh 95 pounds, then drink less). Drink some in the morning, some at lunch, some for the mid afternoon slump, and some for dinner. This juice, if refrigerated, will stay fresh all day long. If you're using one of the slow RPM juicers, it will last two, even three days.

- **Juice one ounce of wheatgrass per day.** Add a bit more each week. If you can't find wheatgrass, add more super green foods, such as blue green algae.

- **Take each of your habitual foods,** the ones you normally consume, and replace them with an alternative fuel that is easier on your body. If you normally have cold cereal and cow's milk in the morning, replace this with a whole grain porridge, such as hot brown rice or millet, prepared the night before, perhaps mixed with dried apricots and raisins. If you normally drink coffee, start tapering down the first ten days, and replacing with alternatives. If you normally have to eat candy bars during the afternoon, replace that with more fresh juice, an apple and a pint or two of water.

- **Eat one to four cloves of raw garlic per day.** Garlic will be your "sickness guard" for the duration of the NACHO. There is no more powerful anti-fungal, anti-bacteria, anti-viral, and anti-parasitic food on the planet. If you skip this step, your chances of "down time" increase. We'll show you ways of getting garlic into your system in the *Recipes* section.

- **Use supplements that supply you with the 3 Rs: probiotics, enzymes, and mineral-rich super greens (such as wild blue green algae, spirulina, and Chlorella). Start slow and increase it over the four weeks.

Drink a freeze-dried green drink. There are many to choose from online and in health food stores. Sprinkle it on a salad, put into a dressing, or mix in with a glass of water or juice.

• Cook up one gaggle of leafy greens each day. Choose from the following: kale, collards, dandelion, or mustard greens.

• Each day, season some of your meals with mineral-dense *Celtic Gray sea salt,* purchased at *The Grain & Salt Society.* Read the testimonials of a simple salt and water program at Dr. Batmanghelidjat's site, *www.watercure2.com.*

• Each morning, fill your hydration jug with at least half your body weight in ounces (if you weigh 100 pounds, drink a minimum of 50 ounces; if 150 pounds, drink 75 ounces). Drink all of this water from your jug each day. If you wish, alkalize your water with a 1/8 to 1/4 teaspoon of organic sea salt per quart or two of water. Lemon is also a great alkalizing agent. Read about the importance of water at the *www.watercure2.com* site.

• Each day, do something for the cleansing and strengthening of your bowels, from an herbal and fiber mix to colonics, to viscera massage.

• Do at least one of the seven Physical Transformers (read the chapter on these), such as skin brushing, saunas, alkaline bath, deep tissue bodywork, and cardiovascular sweating.

• Avoid placing anything chemically artificial on your body. One of the ways we absorb toxins into our body is through chemical deodorants, perfumes, shampoos, mouthwash, toothpaste, and skin creams. These can actually accumulate in your tissues, and cleansing participants will often smell them coming out, especially with the use of saunas and deep body work. Find alternatives. Check out the suggestions listed in the resources section.

Toxic cellular wastes and metabolic residues are very acidic and need the buffering action of proper hydration, alkalization, and simply keeping the sludge moving and moving out. To avoid getting symptoms from the massive amount of cellular exchange taking place, do not overlook these daily regimens. If you do not pay attention to this, you will experience one or more of the detoxification discomforts (mentioned earlier) that you could easily have prevented.

One thing that I find being asked over and over again is questions such as, "Wasn't it hard to do the cleanse? What do you do if you don't like wheat grass, or this thing, or that? What, in heaven's name, can you eat?!" My simple answer is: use your imagination! Experiment - there are so many beautiful options, recipes, and new foods out there.

Karen Ackley Tredwell

What do you eat during your cleanse?

Eating healthy is an essential part of your NACHO program. The key is that you will be making mainly cleansing food choices. Make the primary food intake enzyme rich raw fruits and vegetables and their juices, sprouts, well-chewed seeds and nuts, olive oil, healing soups and broths, cooked whole grain cereals, legumes, and steamed/boiled/sautéed vegetables, seasoned with Celtic Gray sea salt and herbs. Choose whole, unprocessed foods. Select organic foods when possible, especially anything that you will be running through your juicer.

Stop eating foods with additives and preservatives. If you really need to pick up your bacon habit after the four weeks are up, fine. But not during the NACHO.

Since the question always comes up, a quick note on whole grains. **Most people who say they can't eat "grains" are in fact referring to white flour goo. Very few are referring to quinoa, millet, grouts, rye, and buckwheat. They are basing their statement on decades and decades of eating cookies, Italian pasta dishes, crackers, noodles, lasagna, power bars, cakes, and muffins. It is no wonder people say that they "can't eat carbohydrates." This is akin to saying you can't eat oranges because orange soda gives you a stomachache. Flour products are not grains; they're flour.**

So, *whole grains* is not referring to rolled, steel-cut, bleached, or otherwise denatured and beat up flour, even if "it's organic and has the bran and six vitamins put back in." For the full list of great grains and how to prepare them, see Joanne Saltzman's *Amazing Grains*, and other cookbooks listed in the Resources section.

Get your oil needs from olive oil, nuts, seeds, such as flax, psyllium, etc.

Put as much garlic, ginger, cayenne, wild blue green algae, wheatgrass, and pure water as you can put down your gullet.

FOODS TO SLOW DOWN OR ELIMINATE

PROCESSED MEAT: highly processed beef, chicken, lamb, sausages, pate, luncheon meats, bologna

MOST SEAFOODS: bottom feeders, such as mussels, clams, lobster, and highly processed ones, such as anchovies and sardines

PASTEURIZED DAIRY: milk, butter, cheese, ice cream, yogurt, frozen yogurt

PROCESSED OIL: hydrogenated, lard, canola

FLOUR PRODUCTS: bread, pastries, cookies, cakes, pies, donuts, crackers

CAFFEINE: coffee, black teas

TAP WATER: time to get a filter, or bottled spring water

ALCOHOL: beer, wine, sake, scotch, gin, vodka

PROCESSED SUGAR: candy, ice cream, cake, sweets, chocolate

SODAS: coke, diet coke, sugared drinks

FAKE FOODS: artificial anything, diet anything

Daily Schedule

It is impossible to plan out the daily eating schedule for every NACHO participant, given that we are all different, have different cleansing goals, and diverse lifestyles and metabolisms. If you're an extremely active person, running and biking and rock climbing on a regular basis, and in fairly good health, you probably won't be doing the same daily eating schedule as someone who works at home, is comparatively sedentary, and needs an immense increase in their health. If you leave for your office deep in the city at 7 am, and don't return till 6 pm, you'll be planning out your daily eating schedule different than someone who works at home and can get into the kitchen for a quick mid-morning smoothie.

ANIMAL FOOD OR 100 PERCENT PLANT-BASED?

Another large question to factor into ones daily cleansing program is: **some animal food or 100% plant-based diet?** Classically, cleansing programs have recommended using a mainly vegan diet during the cleanse (the word vegan here means "no animal products"). This makes sense: a plant-based diet is very easy to digest, is very low on the food chain, and usually contains many elements that are known cell cleansers (such as chlorophyl). On the other hand, animal products (eggs, fish, meat) are complex building foods, are quite high on the food chain, and often leave behind a large amount of metabolic waste that the body has to deal with.

If you have never eaten a completely 100% plant-based diet (in other words, you have never gone 28 days without animal products), I'm going to suggest you do an plant-based cleanse. Not because it's right or wrong, but simply as part of your cleansing experiment. No one will know the results until you try it.

At the same time, some people don't do as well on a completely plant-based diet as others. For instance, if you are a personal trainer or marathon runner who burns more calories than most of the people in your neighborhood combined, you may find that you get too weak without some animal protein.

If you decide to keep some animal foods in your diet during your cleanse, use the purest and cleanest sources that you can find—i.e., without contamination, drugs, antibiotics, or cruelty.

Now let's lay out one possible scenario for an overall daily eating schedule:

MORNING

Drink a glass of water upon rising. You are seldom more dehydrated than the minute you wake up. You are seldom more acidic than when you first wake up, as well. I like to add a half teaspoon of Celtic gray sea salt to my first glass of water as well.

Make a quart or two of the following:

Half carrot, one quarter beet, one quarter apples/apple juice, or other fruit. You won't be drinking all of it at one sitting, but this will become your "Core" juice for the day.

One tablespoon of a green drink

Consume something with the Three Rs supplementation (ReMineralizing, ReBacterializing, ReEnzymizing)

Eat the food you need to eat. If you normally skip breakfast, then just do the juicing. If you're used to a sweet breakfast, try a fresh fruit smoothie, or bowl of Overnight Oatmeal, for instance, with dried fruit/ One example: two cups oat groats (not oat flakes or cut oats, but whole oats), 1/8 cup flax seed, 1/4 teaspoon of Celtic gray sea salt, and six cups of water. Just before going to bed, bring this to boil, then simmer at the lowest temp possible. It's best to use those two dollar metal filter grate thingies that you put under the pot, to help lower the temperature even more. Wake up in the morning to hot, whole food goodness. Add some dark grade maple syrup, et voilà.

If you normally eat high protein, like bacon and eggs, try rice, beans, and fresh, raw salsa. The key, especially the first week or two, is to match up your normal eating patterns with something that works more as a cleansing food. Remember: you are easing in and resetting the default button on your taste buds.

2 to 5 enzyme capsules

Remember: eat enough. You will make lousy decisions on low fuel. Do NOT go hungry.

MID MORNING

More of your juice. Same juice, or something different.

More water. If you are not urinating every hour or so, your chances of experiencing cleansing symptoms are much greater.

Handful of nuts or seeds, some veggie snacks, a piece of fruit.

Remember, there is no faster way to failure than to *get hungry*. I've yet to meet anyone capable of making great dietary choices once they're starved and low on blood sugar. So keep fueled throughout the day with cleansing foods.

Your colon herb and cleansing product.

LUNCH

More water.

More juice.

Eat lunch. The more raw and enzymatically alive, the better.

A piece or three of Nature's Path *Essene* bread, from their organic Manna line (try their Millet Rice, Multigrain, Sun Seed, or Whole Rye). This is the only "bread" suggested for the NACHO cleanse. As you'll see, it's not really bread, but organic grain sprouts squished together. In my opinion there is no finer Essene bread on the market than Nature's Path (It's keeps well when frozen).

Bowl of one of the Healing Soups (see Recipes).

2 to 5 Enzyme capsules.

Remember: eat enough. Do NOT go hungry.

MID-AFTERNOON

More water.

Another 8-12 ounces of your juice.

Light snack.

DINNER

Leafy green dish (see Recipes).

Any number of the recipes listed in Christina Pirello's *Cooking The Whole Foods Way*, or other whole food cookbooks.

Consume something with the Three Rs supplementation (ReMineralizing, ReBacterializing, ReEnzymizing)

2 to 5 Enzyme capsules

End the day with a warm tea, sweetened with real maple syrup.

Remember: eat enough. Do NOT go hungry.

Overall strategies for each week

The main tenet of the NACHO cleanse— and I think the reason behind its high level of participant success—is KEEPING IT SIMPLE. Doing the program as described above is enough to get results. If you want a focal point for each of the four weeks, however, here are some suggestions:

WEEK ONE

Week One is all about easing in, and resetting the default button on your taste buds. Get used to a new regimen. Go easy on yourself and get warmed up. Taper down the habitual mucus-forming, heavily processed and heavily sugared foods. Stay inspired with the booklets and videos; listen to the tapes in your car. Set up and keep up your new required food chain: do not go anywhere without a NACHO food source, or a gallon of water. You need to drink more water this week than you may have ever had to drink before.

WEEK TWO

Week Two is about increased elimination. Your body is now dumping massive amounts of old cells and metabolic waste material out of your body, through every means necessary (bowels, kidneys, skin, liver, etc.). Focus this week on helping your system speed up this process. Use the colon cleansing methods, including colonics. Increase your use of the Seven Physical Transformers. You need to be sweating at least 3 times this week.

WEEK THREE

Week Three can be considered **Organ Week**. If you're interested in a more intense cleanse, take a look at the one to five day Liver and Kidney/Bladder nutritional cleanses suggested by Dr. Richard Schulze (*There Are No Incurable Diseases*) and Dr. Hulda Regehr Clark (*The Cure of All Cancers*). They're easy to do, and even more powerful in their end result if done midway during a cleansing program. Or, simply continue with a more robust cleansing of the intestinal tract, as in Week Two.

WEEK FOUR

Week Four is **Creating New Habits Week.** The saying is that it takes 21 days to break a habit, or create a new one. You have just past that 21st day. What habits have you erased? What new ones did you create? Think about it for a moment: you just did what most people only dream of. You **changed**. Cement that thought into your brain and thought process. Imagine how your life will turn out differently with these new, healthier habits.

Recipes

One of the realizations that came out of creating the NACHO cleanse was seeing how few NACHO participants knew how to prepare food beyond the 15 or 20 meals they had learned from their mom or college dorm mates. I would get questions like, "If you don't use chicken bouillon cubes for the base of your soup, what can you possibly use... the meat bouillon?" "Isn't instant oatmeal the only form it comes in? How do you cook whole oats?" "I've only used canned beans; how do you cook the dry kind and make them taste good?" "How can I eat cereal without milk?"

I'm not criticizing here. I remember thinking the exact same thoughts, that cooking from whole foods was something done only by old grannies from Europe and bread making hippies with nothing but time on their hands. I looked at it with the utmost awe, eyes wide open: "You made that from *scratch?*" Preparing a soup without bouillon cubes was unheard of, maybe even impossible.

Learning to cook the **basic foods of life** is not only crucial, it is easy as well. Many people think preparing good, cleansing, health-providing food is difficult, and takes too much time. This simply isn't true.

It's beyond the scope of this book to list hundreds of recipes; besides, there are too many great cookbooks already out there. Instead, what is important is to do two things: 1) list some of the greater whole food cookbooks and authors in the Resources section near the end of the book; and 2) list the basic tips, and some of the more important foods of a cleanse, to get you going.

Soup Stocks

I am a strong proponent of daily use of healing broths and soups, not only during the NACHO cleanse, but in normal life as well. They are a vastly underrated food source, especially for novices interested in learning how to cook and prepare more of their own meals. They're easy, fun to prepare, a phenomenal way to get superfoods into you (such as garlic, ginger, Celtic Gray sea salt, sea vegetables, etc.), a great way to make use of leftovers from the bottom of your refrigerator, they are best made a gallon or two at a time, and very, very difficult to screw up.

I am also a strong proponent of the "non recipe" approach, done by taste, not by measurement. With that in mind, here are some of the more tasty soup bases.

MODIFIED DASHI—THIN SOUP STOCK

Six inch piece of dried, mineral-rich *kombu* sea vegetable. 1 onion, thinly sliced. 1 cup bean sprouts. Handful of mushrooms (fresh or dried). Natural soy sauce (look for ones called *Shoyu* or *Tamari*). Celtic gray sea salt.

Place kombu in a large saucepan with 2 quarts cold water. Bring to a simmer. Add onions and mushrooms, simmer for another 10 minutes. Add sprouts towards end, then season first with Celtic Gray sea salt and then add some tamari or shoyu until tasty. Strain out the kombu and mushrooms, chop them both up into smaller pieces, then put back in, along with the sprouts.

CLASSIC MISO STOCK

One of the surest ways to get an audible, healing sigh out of dinner guests at the Ohlgren household is to serve simple miso soup. There is an unmistakable internal sense that, with each sip, you are doing something good for your health.

Miso is a extraordinary source of concentrated nutrition. Made by fermenting soybeans for up to two years, miso is an excellent source of assimilable amino acids, minerals, vitamins, fiber, good lactic acid, bacteria, and enzymes (holy moly, the Three Rs!). It has long been considered a medicinal food, used for lowering cholesterol, alkalinizing the blood, and neutralizing the effects of smoking and environmental pollution. Find and use only real, long fermented, **non-pasteurized** miso. Any flavor will do. It is generally found in the refrigerated section.

The key to good miso is to add the paste towards the end of preparation. You'll need about a tablespoon or two of miso paste per quart of water. Thin the miso paste by adding enough water to make it soupy, then set it aside. Boil a quart of water, bring to a simmer, add a few thinly sliced spring/green onions, then the miso to taste. You'll know when you have the taste right, because it invariably elicits the miso *"ahhh"* sound from you and your guests.

This is the simplest form of miso soup, and like Dashi, it can be served by itself, or used as the base stock for many other varieties of soups.

Sautéed Base

Pour olive oil in a large frying pan. Cut two onions (yellow, red, white, green) into small 1/4" pieces (celery is good, too), stir into the oil. Add a teaspoon of any number of herbs, such as sage, oregano, thyme, pepper, etc. Cover, and simmer for fifteen minutes until soft. This can be added to any soup, either before or after the soup has been puréed.

Soup Guts

Take a couple of hard squash, make a slice or hole in each near the top (to allow internal pressure to escape), bake in the oven at 350° for an hour. Cut in half, remove the seeds and most of the outer skin, and place in a quart or so of water (if you don't have time to do these baking steps, skip them and just cut up the squash into cubes). Purée in the pot, using one of those hand held twenty dollar blenders that every NACHO participant should have. Bring to simmer, add vegetables, the Sautéed Base, olive oil and Celtic Gray sea salt to taste.

Take a few cups of cooked beans (any and all will do). Add to a quart or so of water. Purée in the pot, and follow the same directions as above.

Bake or simmer an entire head of cauliflower, broccoli, potatoes (Idaho, sweet, red, etc.), Purée in the pot, and follow the same directions as above.

Take a cup or so of pine nuts (other nuts will work as well, but pine nuts are easy). Place in a jar with one cup of hot water. Purée using a hand held blender, until the consistency of milk. This can become a thickener, poured into any soup.

Juicing tips and recipes

MAKING THE "CORE" JUICE

As a former restaurant chef, I learned early on not to waste time or movement in a kitchen. Because of this, I seldom prepare any food or dish in small portions. Part of this might be because I'm 6'8" and weigh 215 pounds, but the main reason is that I hate wasting time, and I am too busy to spend a lot of time in the kitchen. When I make soup, I make 2 gallons; when I cook a grain, I make 3 quarts of it. Same goes for juicing. There's no way I would ever juice up just 8 ounces of carrots. Although juicers such as the **Kempo Plus Multi-Juice Extractor** mentioned earlier clean up in about 90 seconds, I find it silly to be preparing juice more than once or twice a day.

Because of this method, I've learned to make what I call the "core" juice, refrigerate that, and then add different things to it as needed. This core juice, by itself, is generally too strong for me to drink straight, at least in the volumes of juice I do during a NACHO (I'll often consume a gallon of vegetable juice per day).

The core juice will often consist of carrots, beets, wheat grass sprouts, a bit of fresh ginger root, a few whole lemons or limes (peel and all), and any spare vegetables I have left in the refrigerator.

Since wheatgrass has such a strong taste, I have learned to make it quite tasty by making something called a *Wheat Grasshopper*. See below.

How To Enjoy
Wheatgrass for Years

Wheatgrass juice is extracted from the red wheat berry after it has sprouted and grown for about a week, to 4 to 6 inches tall. This deep green juice is extremely rich in minerals, vitamins, chlorophyll, over 30 types of enzymes, and what could only be called a strong, vital "life force." Benefits are often seen with only one ounce per day. Its healing properties have been the subject of entire books and research, including use as a blood purifier, liver detoxifier, and a positive role in anemia and oxygenation of red blood cells.

Some one has to say it, so I will: **do not drink wheatgrass straight, by itself.**

Before any of you experienced wheatgrass proponents throw down this book and put up your fists, please hear me out. I didn't say "Don't drink it." I'm saying "Don't drink it straight, by itself." The reason is real simple: those that do *stop drinking wheatgrass.*

Don't believe me? Once you're into your NACHO cleanse, juice up a few ounces and offer a triple shot to any long time wheatgrass juicer, and then *watch their facial expression.* You will see someone struggle to not gag. They may drink those shots, but they won't be drinking any more for a long, long time.

Wheatgrass has one of the strongest tastes, at least of anything we juice, of any plant in the world. At first, it can actually be enjoyable, and I've seen many people do daily shots of straight wheatgrass for months, *when they're first introduced to it.* But I know very, very, few proponents of wheatgrass—even the authors who write about its healing and transformative properties!—who continue drinking it after the first 6 to 18 months.

The reason? They *gag* on its taste after a while. Hell, they gag from its smell alone.

I get my trays of wheatgrass from a small group of entrepreneurs located at a farm a few miles down the road. They are young and healthy as can be, but none of them drink shots of wheatgrass anymore. The reason: after years of growing and drinking it, they choke on the taste and smell.

You don't want to get to that point. The juice of wheat sprout is, hands down, among the top 5 most powerful cleansing and health reparative superfoods on earth. After you see what a small amount of daily, or at least weekly, wheatgrass juice can do for your health (I'm talking an ounce or two), you will want to continue using it for years and years, like I have. But there is no way you'll be able to do this if you start out drinking it straight.

It's been decades since I was turned on to wheatgrass, and I can still consume 10 or 12 shots a day during a cleanse. It is not that I'm immune to its smell and taste. The secret is that I always mix it with lemon and apple juice. These *wheat grasshoppers* taste like strong lemonade. I've served 8 ounce glasses to real meat and potato friends, and they will often ask for more. Why and how the sour of the lemon and the characteristics of the apple juice balance the taste so well is beyond my food chemistry skills, I just know it works. And it can all be done with one juicer, at the same time:

> 1 lemon (rind and all, just cut it so it fits in the juicer)
>
> Enough wheatgrass for one ounce
>
> Enough apples/ raw apple juice to bring the full amount up to 6-8 ounces.

If the taste is not delicious, add more lemon, or add more apple, or a few carrots.

Last note on wheatgrass: the juice from wheat sprouts is a completely different creature than the flour from wheat berries. This is important for those who feel that they are allergic to wheat and wheat flour. You will not have any allergic response to wheatgrass juice. You may well have a health producing *cleansing response,* but not an allergic one.

MAKE IT ALL TASTE GOOD

One of the biggest errors I see people make when it comes to both healthy food and healthy juices is in regards to taste. If the food/juice you make and consume isn't down right delectable, you will only consume it for a short period of time, and then probably never again. Given that we're trying to develop life long habits, this is a mistake. Sure, when and while your taste buds are damaged from years and years of junk food, hydrogenated fat and sugar, there's not a lot of room in the alternative taste department; pretty much everything outside of McDonald's tastes lousy. But as you start resetting the taste bud button, you'll find that there are ways, especially with fresh juice, that make the difference between a lousy tasting juice, and a great one. Here are some hints:

Regulate the amount of bitter. Out of the five main tastes in food—sweet, salty, sour, spicy, and bitter— bitter is the taste most missing from a standard American diet, and for good reason: it's the one taste that is most difficult for those with a mucus laden, sugar coated inner terrain. But bitter foods are critical for many of our organs, so one of the purposes of a juice-based cleansing program is to put the bitter taste back into our foods. The key is to keep the amount of bitter in the range where it doesn't overpower the sweetness and good taste of the juice. Some of the bitter juicing vegetables are parsley, kale, collards, and wheatgrass.

Serve chilled. Don't be afraid of a little ice or at least cooler temperatures. Lukewarm carrot juice will not make (or keep!) any new cleansing converts.

Don't overdo the food combining theory. One of the more valid and life enhancing ideas that is embraced in nutritional healing is *food combining* (eating protein and fruit separately, for example). However, one of the areas that I disagree with on most food-combining charts is their suggestion to never mix fruit with vegetables. Perhaps as a cooked dish, but I have not found too many people that suffer from a combination of raw veggies and raw fruit. They seem to digest fine together; they certainly taste great. Give it a try.

No juice is irreparable. If you ever come up with a juice combination that tastes horrendous, DON'T throw it out. Simply add enough apple juice, and perhaps a lemon, until it is tasty once again.

SOME JUICE RECIPES

Below are some ideas for juice combinations and recipes. As you'll soon guess, exact measurements are not my forte or my preferred style —I've never measured any juice ingredient in my life. And this is not intended to be a recipe book. These ideas below are simply to get you started. There are many recipes that can be found in juicing books, as well as a search online; www.google.com is still the best search engine by far.

Scrub the dirt off your veggies. In general, peeling isn't necessary. Cut out bruised and damaged areas, and then chop into pieces that easily go into your juicer's hopper. Save a couple carrots or other hard root vegetables as the last thing you juice through; this will help grab any remaining fibers of softer foods you've been juicing (such as lemon and other fruit).

Feel free to experiment by adding small amounts of ginger, garlic, green drink mix, a sprig of parsley, lemon, burdock root, wheatgrass or sweet potato to your juices.

Baseline

> 12 carrots
> 4 apples
> 3 celery sticks
> touch of parsley

Enzyme Mainline

> 6 carrots
> 2 pears
> 1/2 to one whole pineapple
> 1 ounce of wheatgrass
> 1 lemon

Refresher Course

> 3 apples
> 10 carrots
> 1 lemon

Holiday Rush

> 6 apples

1 large bunch of grapes
handful of parsley
1 whole lemon
1 inch fresh ginger root

Kidney Kleanser

10-12 carrots
3 beets
1 cup red cabbage
bit of parsnip and turnip
6 celery stalks
3 red radishes (or 1 inch daikon radish)
3 or 4 tart apples
cup of frozen/fresh unsweetened cranberries

Whoa...

10-12 carrots
5 celery stalks
2 cloves of garlic
large handful of parsley

Potassium City

Cup of kale
Cup of parsley
Cup of celery
Cup of carrots

Some of the Superfoods

LEAFY GREENS

Wash one bunch of greens. Remove the fibrous lower stem (this is optional; you can leave them on if cooked longer, or chopped finely and placed in a soup). Either steam or cover the greens in water and boil until tender (5-15 minutes). Remove, and cut up. Serve hot or cold. Mix with premixed olive oil, lemon, and Celtic Gray sea salt dressing. Sprinkle with a few raw or toasted nuts, and very finely chopped red onion. Done correctly, this is a dish that you'll never get tired of.

I've added some ginger pieces to the water before cooking, and then used this green and nutritious leftover liquid as a night time tea. Add a bit of tamari for taste, or drink it plain.

One caveat: some leafy greens are fairly high in oxalic acid, namely spinach, swiss chard, rhubarb, and sorrel. While fine in small amounts, oxalic acid can bind with important nutrients, particularly iron and calcium, making them inaccessible, and has been linked to irritation of the digestive system, kidney stones, arthritis, and gout. Small portions are fine, **but make your main leafy greens those of the cabbage family, such as kale and collards.**

ALGAE: MASTERS OF REGENERATION

To a society raised on iceberg lettuce and the vegetable known as "ketchup", the thought of putting algae into ones food chain has as much appeal as cod liver oil ice cream. But for those who know, algae can be not only be delectable, they *have* been delectable for thousands of years.

Here are some excerpts from the new book, **How Health Works:** *The Movement For Nutritional Sanity*—

According to the National Wildlife Foundation, there are 26,900 known species of algae in the world and more are being discovered every year (for the record, algae are plural; alga is singular; there is no such word as algaes). Fossilized algae have been found that are more than 3 billion years old, which dates them to a time when the earth's crust hadn't cooled and the main atmospheric component was still carbon dioxide. It was algae that first figured out how to essentially eat light. Using carbon dioxide, minerals, and sunlight, this handy trick of photosynthesis was what converted the atmosphere into the useable one we now breathe. Depending on their particular light diet, algae will generally be blue-green, green, red, brown, or golden in color and classification, with blue green algae being the first and oldest.

Many people think that trees are the main creators of O_2. They're not. Algae are still the source of 80% of the world's oxygen supply.

Algae form the base starting point of nearly every food chain. They can thrive in a wide variety of environments, from the soil in your back yard, to the bottoms of the ocean and fresh water lakes, to the green ones that grow on your fish tank glass, and ones that can live deep in thermal hot springs.

Algae have had as long of a human consumption record as its terrestrial cousins. By all accounts, they've been a significant source of food since man's beginning. *"There is archeological evidence that the Aztecs cultivated Spirulina in several lakes as well as in the intricate Mayan water-ways of southern Mexico. In the Near East during Biblical times, the food Manna was prepared with the Nostoc species of microalgae. Washed onto the shore of lakes, it would be collected by women and sun-dried. This is still carried out today by the Kanembu natives along the shores of Lake Johan in Chad in the deep African Sahara; they prepare buns with it or drink it as a spicy soup."* (Peter Holmes, The Energetics of Western Herbs Volume One.) Evidence of algae use has also been found in Paleolithic burial grounds, Viking records, and American Indian sea-shore and fresh water lake tribal lore. In Japan, marine algae —such as hiziki, arame, and wakame— as well as lake algae, like Chlorella, still represent almost a quarter of the total food intake.

Out of the ocean group of algae, *"most of them are red (6000 species), brown (2000 species) or green (1200 spe-cies). None are known to be poisonous,"* says professor Michael Guiry, Ph.D., Head of the Department of Botany at the National University of Ireland, and author of A Consensus and Bibliography of Irish Seaweeds.

Having eaten both fresh water & marine algae dishes daily for the past 18 years, I can attest that the only thing odd about them is us. We are simply one of the few cultures that haven't gotten in on the act.

Both wild and cultivated sources of clean, organically grown, food-grade algae are still quite available. Large quantities of Spirulina platensis are now aqua-farmed from large man-made ponds in regions like China, India, Thailand, and California. Wild Aphanizomenon flos-aqua, a naturally occurring blue green algae, has been harvested during its growing season since the early eighties from the only farmable source known, the waters of Upper Klamath Lake, Oregon. Chlorella, a fresh-water green algae, has been successfully cultivated in ponds since the fifties, mainly in Japan. Ocean aquaculture farmers along the more isolated coastlines of Ireland, Japan, and both American coasts supply the world with millions of pounds of wild-crafted sea vegetables each year.

Some algae are capable of binding with heavy metals and other environmental chemicals stored in our fat cells, allowing these to be eliminated through the gastrointestinal tract. Japan and Russia researchers have long known of the heavy metal detoxification abilities of algae, notably cadmium, lead, and mercury. After the Chernobyl nuclear reactor accident in 1986, Russian scientists used a Siberian coastal brown algae, known for its rich source of alginates, as an effective and edible absorber of heavy metals and radioactive elements for those who had been exposed to the radiation.

Where algae become interesting to us though, especially with respect to the topic of cellular regeneration, is in their extraordinary track record on physical health. Probably the most thorough compilation of this record ever done is by Dr. Jeffrey Bruno, Ph.D. In his *Edible Microalgae—A Review of the Health Research*, Bruno cites several hundred scientific peer-reviewed references on marine and fresh water edible algae, dividing them into eleven therapeutic categories, as far-reaching and diverse as increased brain function, improved cellular repair, cancer protective effects, allergy and asthma relief, and their overall detoxification properties.

Sort of the "Desktop Reference" for algae uses, Bruno's book cites enough scientific research to fill a small library. A reader becomes aware that algae have been shown to inhibit tumor growth and can reduce cholesterol; some have anti-cancer, brain and sensory nerve benefits; others are natural antibiotics, and help support glandular health (especially the pituitary, thyroid, and adrenal glands). There is an entire section on the radiation protective effects alone. Algae have been shown to be effective with herpes-simplex. At least six research studies showed improvements in children's cognition, mood, behavior, and academic performance.

Bruno also reports on the more mundane effects of eating marine and fresh water algae, such as increased energy and vitality, lessoning of cold and flu symptoms, balanced mood swings, reduced stress, reduction of anxiety and depression, and improved memory and concentration.

Few other plants have as many healing properties connected with them as algae. And, virtually no other group of plants is capable of holding as many trace minerals as well. Ocean and mountain lake seaweeds can contain upwards of 60 and even 70 trace and rare earth elements, more than any plant found on the earth. That's about as many elements from the Periodic Table that are known to be needed for human health.

Nutritional analysis of most edible seaweed reads like the Holy Grail of every supplement company's dream pill. What algae contain is what all supplements wish they did. They are a high level source of amino acids (Chlorella, Spirulina, and wild blue green algae are 50-70% protein) in profiles often similar to human blood; vitamins, including beta carotene, C, E, K, and the hard-to-find B-12, are in most algae, along with the co-factors that actually make them absorbable. Dunaliella, a wild red ocean algae harvested off the coast of New Zealand, contains one of the highest sources of beta-carotene found in any plant in the world. Algae are low in calories and unexpectedly low in sodium as well—most of the salt in marine algae are found on its powdery surface, easily removed by rinsing and soaking. In my opinion, they truly are the world's best "vitamin pill".

Over the last few years, Blue Green Algae have become one of the most highly researched plants. It has been studied at McGill University, the University of New Mexico, and Oregon State University.

The main focus and findings of these studies is the positive impact of BG Algae on our immune and nervous systems. The McGill study in particular shows that after eating Aphanizomenon flos-aqua, there is a 40% increase of Natural Killer Cells in the blood, a recognized sign of a strengthened immune system.

I was lucky to be introduced to sea vegetables in my early twenties, in meals prepared by world class chefs. From that very first bite of an *Arame and Carrot Sauté* dish, I was hooked. I felt that I'd been looking for this food all my life. Unfortunately, very few cooks know how to prepare sea algae in a scrumptious way, which is why many people don't think of them as delicious. You haven't really lived, though, until you've been served wild-crafted *Sea Palm and Jicama Salad* with fresh squeezed lemon, olive oil, oregano, and sea salt dressing.

And remember, eating algae are not so bizarre. We're simply one of the last cultures to do so.

Sea vegetables are easy to prepare. They can be rinsed and simply thrown into a root stew. You can toast a handful of Sea Palm (*Eisenia arborea*) in the oven for ten minutes, and have a crunchy snack that wows guests and beats potato chips hands down. Many new, prepared sea vegetable snacks are on the market. There are instant wakame flakes for soups, and smoked dulse as an alternative to chips. You can buy or learn to make great *gomasio* (crushed sesame seeds and sea salt) by adding toasted arame or sea palm into it. And, for a tangy condiment, try pickled kelp.

One of my favorite desserts is a fresh fruit and juice dessert gel, thickened with the clear seaweed called *agar*. It beats our mom's generation of gelatin in terms of flavor and nutrients. It certainly beats it in terms of origin (gelatin is made from horse and cow hooves).

There are too many great whole food cookbooks out there for me to start giving recipes here. I'd rather introduce you to these chefs and their work, which I do in the section called *Books to Wear Out*. But look for recipes that contain these wild-crafted species:

Kombu (*Laminaria*), for centuries it was added to bean dishes as a tenderizer, long before anyone figured out that it was the amino acid glutamate (similar to MSG, without the side effects) that was behind this action.

Nori (*Porphyra*), **Wakame** (*Undaria*), two of the more well-known sea vegetables. Wakame is great in salad.

Arame (*Eisenia bicyclis*). Delicious and high in B-12.

Sea Palm, probably my all time favorites from the American Pacific coastline. Its mild taste and *al dente* texture make it the one I usually start out and serve to algae virgins.

Dulse, Laver and **Kelp**. Naturally rich in *symbiosed* iodine, potassium and other minerals related to thyroid functions, and associated with the relief of rheumatism and rheumatoid arthritis.

Hiziki is a powerhouse of nutrition. When I'm feeling depleted, it is this particular sea vegetable that I cook up. A very rich and satisfying taste.

Fresh Water Algae: Because of their small size and texture, fresh water **Green Algae** (*Chlorella Pyrenoidosa*) and **Blue Green Algae** (spirulina *arthrospira platensis* and the wild-crafted *aphanizomenon flos-aqua*, or AFA) don't appear in many recipes, other than as an additional ingredient added to smoothies, breads, and the growing popularity of green drinks. But having personally consumed wild-crafted AFA blue green algae every single day for the past 14 years, and being familiar with the remarkable amount of research that has been done on chlorella, spirulina, and AFA, I was glad to see Dr. Bruno's book make so many references to the health benefits associated with them. For instance, children eating AFA showed a *"dramatic improvement in class"*. Another children's study *"demonstrated a superior immune response"*. He also reports on the findings of immunologist Gitte Jensen, Ph.D. at McGill University, who showed in repeated testing with AFA an *"improved trafficking of immune cells"*, a good sign of immune system strength. In a follow-up study, she also noted that *"high doses of AFA were not required to realize these benefits. The positive immune response was seen with as low as 1.5 grams of AFA."* In 1989, the National Cancer Institute reported that a number of blue green algae extracts were found to be *"remarkably active against the AIDS virus."*

For people on the go, who don't have the opportunity to prepare healthy meals, there is no easier, more efficient way to remineralize your body than with fresh water algae.

GARLIC

Dr. Richard Schulze, one of the preeminent natural healers in America, and a personal hero of mine, says it best in his book, *There Are No Incurable Diseases: "If you use only one herb, it should be garlic. It is a powerful broad spectrum antibiotic... it is also anti-viral, anti-fungal, anti-parasitic and has proven itself to rid the body internally and externally of any antigens or pathogens. Garlic has been proven in hospitals and laboratories worldwide to destroy cancer and break up tumors, thin the blood and normalize blood pressure and cholesterol levels."*

Many cleansing aficionados and authors suggest putting raw garlic in one's juices. I disagree; the taste is so strong that after a while, it adds to people's disdain for regular cleansing and destroys their love of fresh juice. Besides, there are just too many ways to add raw garlic into food dishes that are nothing short of mouth-watering. My recommendation: get fresh garlic into your system through other ways than your juice.

Because of the critical role that garlic plays in the NACHO (with 2-6 raw cloves per day), there are two must-have tools I recommend: the *Garlic Peeler*, and a *garlic press*.

The Garlic Peeler is an ingenious $7 surgical tube-looking gadget made for easily peeling garlic cloves, so simple in its design that it has elicited millions of "I should have come up with this!" thoughts for millions of first time users. I've yet to meet anyone blasé about this tool. No more garlic-smelling hands, and no more painstaking peeling. You'll wonder how you lived without it.

The other tool is the $10-$20 garlic press, for quickly adding a minced clove or two to your meals. Add them to your soup, right at the end, just before serving. Blend up 8 cloves of peeled garlic with 6 ounces of olive oil, any fresh herb (such as rosemary, basil, oregano, thyme) the juice of one lemon, and enough salt for taste. Add over brown rice or millet. Or brush onto a piece of *Essene bread,* and lightly toast.

If I'm in a hurry, I will also simply cut a couple cloves up into pieces about the size of a capsule, and swallow them with water, in the same way I swallow my algae each day.

How and where to learn more

Recipes and food preparation ideas could and do take up whole cookbooks. Instead of competing with the brilliant ones already out there, I am going to suggest the cookbooks that I learned from. Start with the ones listed in the the back of this book.

Do you have recipes to suggest? Please do, by posting them on the NACHO chat list, and share your thoughts with others at www.howhealthworks.com/forum/.

Other ideas:

Take a cooking class. Check out the schools and local cooks on the HHW site, under the Resources link. School of Natural Cookery suggested in the Resources. Read books. Cook with friends. Learn how to prepare real, life-giving food.

Get nutritional counseling. If you're battling with procrastination or fear or just plain apathy, or you have a particular set of symptoms, contact one of the nutritional counselors on the HHW site. These are all people who understand cleansing and healing from personal experience. Here are two:

Russell Mariani, M.D. - www.HealthEquest.com
514 Amherst Road, South Hadley, MA 01075
413 536-0275

Ginny Harper - www.KiOfLife.com
106 Seminole Drive, Franklin, TN 37064
615 646-2841

Previously, even when I slept 7 or 8 hours, I would awaken feeling like my night's rest had been cut short. However, it was more typical to wake up frequently during the night; sometimes I'd fall back to sleep in a rather fitful fashion. It was more common to be awake for the rest of the night. Consequently, my energy level was extremely low. I'd be able to put in a full day's work but feel like I had no energy left to exercise, or more importantly, spend time with my family. My energy level picked up within a few days of following the cleanse; better, restful sleep soon followed. (In fact, there were times when I almost felt like I had too much energy!) The advice about keeping well-hydrated really assists one from feeling too headachey or fatigued.

Karen Ackley Tredwell

7 Physical Transformers

In the process of learning how to repair and maintain my own health over the years, there are seven methods that I have found to be invaluable, especially during nutritional tune-ups, such as a cleanse.

These 7 *Physical Transformers* are deceptively simple, which is why so many people don't use them. Yet I find myself returning to these cleansing tools over and over since first learning them in the early 1980s. Don't let their simplicity fool you, they are extraordinarily effective.

What are the 7 PTs for?

The seven PTs help cleanse and purge the body, both internally and externally, by keeping the natural pathways of metabolism open. They get our sludge moving! I have personally shortened flu and cold symptoms with many of these tools.

They help move the body's lymph, critical in times of illness.

Skin, skin, skin! Every single one of them helps your skin remain smooth and young. Hair and nails, too.

They revitalize your energy. If I find myself overtired, I find I start adding these 7 PTs back into my routine.

They lower stress levels, and give a noticeable jump in mental clarity.

They rebalance the inner terrain. Recently been on a sugar binge? Too much Road Food lately? Do The 7 PTs.

How to tell if you need the 7 PTs

For some, it is a physical feeling. You start becoming aware of when you feel sludgy... or toxic... or your skin itches, or you feel mucosy, you feel like you need a shower when you just took one 3 hours ago.

For others, it's mainly visual: you look in the mirror one morning, and say, "Scott, it's time to clean up your act, buddy." Puffiness of the face and tissues, redness around the nose, pupils lose their white color, or the classic dark circles under the eyes, are all visual signs worthy of the Seven PTs.

Another sign of the need for the PTs is body scents. We've all experienced our body flowering differently than ones normal range. Smells are one of the surest ways of detecting toxicity.

Maintenance. Why wait until you need them to do them? Besides, they're actually fun, and they make you feel alive.

But here's the main reason for doing them religiously during the NACHO: **speeding up your results. Each of the Seven PTs help accelerate the results of cellular regeneration during a cleanse.**

All Seven PTs are explained in detail in volume three of the How Health Works Audio Series, appropriately named *The Seven Physical Transformers,* but here is a brief explanation of each one:

#1 REHYDRATING

This one has already been drilled in, but it's the one most often overlooked. During your 28 days, drink 3 to 4 quarts of pure spring water a day.

One of the important reasons for rehydrating is *lymph.* The lymph system is the often overlooked set of vessels used to transport metabolic waste out of the body. During a cleanse, the lymph system can become overwhelmed with old, necrotic material.

One of the world's top educators and pioneers on live blood cell analysis, Michael Coyle, said it this way to me: *"Overloaded lymph can get like dried up snot."* Lymph can get that slow and thick when loaded down with waste. The best way to get lymph thinned out and flowing again is water. Water is the great solvent of the body (learn more about lymph in the *Real Food, Real Health* audio series).

Chronically dehydrated cells are similar to a jar of dried beans: initially they don't absorb very well; water seems to pass right by them. But after a few days, you'll start to feel like the water is no longer running straight through. The cells are now absorbing, and utilizing, this new volume of solvent H_2O.

Buy a bottle, somewhere around the size of a gallon. This will be your official Rehydration Jug. Fill it each day, and drink it empty each day. It is really the only way you are going to be able to measurably know how much water you are using. Drink at least half your body weight in ounces of water. If you don't have access to spring water, then filter your tap water with a carbon filter.

#2 SKIN BRUSHING

Our skin can be considered our largest elimination organ, especially during a change in nutrition. To help this process along, purchase a long handled skin brush (or rough wash cloth) and dry-brush your entire body for two or three minutes before bathing or showering each day. It may sting a bit the first few times, but you are conditioning your skin to breathe more. This also improves circulation, releases toxins and stimulates new skin cell production. For some, wet-brushing while bathing can be just as effective.

#3 COLON CLEANSING

Much of our health revolves around the condition of our digestive tract. Since there is generally an increase in impurities moving through the intestines during an improvement of nutrition, helping it do its job will vastly improve your results.

Colon Cleansers are a combination of herb and fiber products that can act as both cleansers and intestinal wall strengtheners.

Colon Therapy, also called colonics, is the method of using warm water to gently cleanse the lower portion of the intestinal tract. In twenty years, I've yet to meet any colonic user who doesn't sing its praises. Ask around, and find a good local colon therapist. Have them set up two to four sessions during your NACHO cleanse.

#4 Sauna Rounds

Entire books have been written about the health benefits of saunas. In Sweden, the saying is, "Build your house around the sauna." Saunas are a way to heat the body's temperature and allow it to sweat out excess impurities. Find a health club that has a dry or wet sauna, and go as often as possible. The improvements in your skin alone are worth the trouble. Remember to replace the fluids you lose. Bring your Rehydrating Bottle in the sauna with you.

Like some of the other PTs, most people have been in a sauna before, but few have used them in a guided, cell rejuvenating way. Saunas require some conditioning, in order to get past that "I'm hot and uncomfortable" feeling. This suffering comes about because the skin is *not conditioned…* it's not opening and closing to allow the sweat to flow.

I'm going to teach you a way to use Sauna's that treat the skin like the organ it is: you are going to have living, breathing, fully functioning skin again after you do a few Sauna Rounds.

First, start out with a light skin brushing—this will help a lot to get things going. Now go into the sauna for about 5-10 minutes. Don't worry if you don't break into a full sweat. You'll see how to achieve this in a minute.

Once you're sweating a bit, step out and take a cold shower for about 10-20 seconds. When I mean cold, I mean cold enough that it sort of takes your breath away. It needs to be cold enough so that you want to get back into the sauna. It's only 10 to 60 seconds, but that contraction of the skin, that squeezing of the lymph system, is very important.

That's Round One. Now hop back into the sauna. This time, you'll start to notice something different: you're going to break a sweat faster, and you're going to sweat *more*. Why? Because you are conditioning the skin.

After 5 or 10 minutes, jump out into a 10-20 second cold plunge. Skin brush if you want, then start Round 3.

Work up to where you can do 3 to 5 of these Rounds. If you need to rest between sessions, just lie down outside the sauna for a while. Stay hydrated. Always have plenty of water.

If you find that your skin is not breaking a sweat easily and you are just getting hot without any sweat, no problem. This just means that your skin really needs this. What you'll find is that your skin will eventually start to open up and become more breathable and flexible. Don't worry if this takes a few rounds, or even a few sessions. The main reason people say "I don't like saunas" is because their skin isn't breathing, and they've never done the hot/cold/hot approach.

Owning your own detoxifying and regenerating sauna is no longer a luxury. Like a juicer and other health-giving tools, portable and lightweight Far Infrared saunas are now available and affordable, and can be stored in any apartment closet. The best we've found is the *BioTherm* carbon black Far Infrared dome sauna. For more details, visit the How Health Works website.

#5 ALKALINIZING BATHS

Taking baths are as easy as falling off a log, and many people have done an alkalinizing bath at one time or another. But very few people have done them consistently over the course of a month, and in conjunction with some of these other PTs. This is really where the value comes in. Not once in awhile, but steadily, over the course of 28 days.

The object is to make the outside water more alkaline than

the body and blood itself. It can be done with either inexpensive bulk sea salt or baking soda. Easy, relaxing, and powerful when combined with skin brushing. Three times per week; 1 to 2 cups per bath.

#6 DEEP BODYWORK

Good bodywork is something to behold, and I am forever amazed at the number of people who have never tried it, or budgeted for it. Look for practitioners who come well recommended by people who have seen the results. Shiatsu, Visceral Manipulation, Lymph Drainage, Rolfing, Deep Swedish, and Self-Massage are the types of bodywork to consider during a cleanse. Each of these methods can improve circulation, elimination, and help stimulate the lymph system.

One of the tenets of a cleanse is: *Move things around. Get organs and lymph and stagnation moving.* Although light oil massage, and other more energetic type of bodywork can be perfect for other times, a cleanse works best with deeper, more physically moving work. You are looking for bodywork that shakes up the pattern and *moves things around.*

#7 CARDIOVASCULAR WORKOUT

If you are already exercising, then all of the benefits are known to you. If you are like me though, and not a naturally inclined workout person, I want to add some new inspiration that has worked wonders in getting me and keeping me fit, and that's the recognition that all of the things that have been mentioned in this book are doubled in effectiveness when you work your heart and lungs: getting your lymph flowing like a river (instead of like a swamp), getting your intestines to move better and not build up toxicity; improving the condition of your skin; lowering the stress of life. I have seen improvements with all of these simply by doing some *physical action* a few times a week, even 15-20 minutes 3 times a week.

Daily moderate exercise promotes psychological well-being and self-esteem. It reduces feelings of depression and anxiety, helps manage weight loss, and helps build and make healthy bones, muscles and joints. 20 minutes—enough to break a sweat—a few times each week will accelerate your NACHO success.

Rule One: Find a partner or get a coach. I speak from experience. Since I am "aerobically challenged", I either have a friend with whom I walk/run/work out, or I hire a trainer to keep me in the gym.

Rule Two: If you are depressed, **move**. There. Is. No. Depression. In. Movement.

Try it—try staying in the exact same mental state you were in before a jog up the street, or 30 minutes in the gym. It doesn't work. Sweat not only gives you a new perspective, it also changes your body chemistry. Those that tell me that they're "chemically depressed" are unaware of who the chemist is.

Make it easy: Write in your daily schedule when you will be physically active; make an appointment with yourself, and treat it like a real appointment. That's how I do it.

On coffee or lunch breaks, take a brisk 5-10 minute walk around the building.

Take walks where you breathe deeply. Dr. Richard Schulze, one of the top natural healers in America, says it simply: "Fresh air will help you heal faster."

NACHO Tips

Costs involved with the NACHO

As mentioned earlier, human beings have been doing nutritional cleanses for thousands of years, long before the terms *supplements, colon therapy, deep bodywork,* and *superfood* were around. It is possible to do a very inexpensive, downright cheap, cellular cleanse. **If you can afford clean water and a few dollars for vegetables, you can do this program and get amazing results.**

However, think for a moment about the range of silly items on which we humans can spend our hard-earned money ($4 daily cappuccinos come to mind), then couple that with the far reaching effects that these 28 days can have on the rest of your life. Given that, I strongly suggest taking some of your income and budgeting it towards your cleansing program. Take that coffee budget and put it towards the superfoods suggested. Put probiotics and enzymes into your digestive tract to revitalize your digestion. Find an affordable bodywork; work out trades; borrow a juicer; buy in bulk… you get the idea: *invest in yourself* for 28 days. It will come back to you in spades.

If you are having a hard time

During your NACHO program, if you start having a hard time, I am 99% sure that it is because of the same three things I see over and over:

1. You are feeling the effects of detoxification. Rarely does someone escape the effects of **old cell burn off** during a cleanse. There are some very effective tricks that have been shared in this book, but your biggest ally during detox may well be your *brain*. You must understand that what your body is going through is not only normal, but healthy. On the other side of detox is a level of health you haven't been at in years, perhaps decades.

2. You're not sleeping enough, nor drinking enough. During the NACHO cleanse, you are going through the process of healing. I would suggest that this healing is deeper, and more profoundly impactful, than any healing you've experienced to date. You need more rest than you normally need. This isn't the time to be staying out late at night, or keeping your normal hours. For the first couple weeks of your cleanse, plan your days so that you have more down time. Also, if you're not drinking at least *half your weight in ounces of water,* the removal of old sludge and cells will take longer. A cleanse is a time when our lymph system is running at full capacity, removing old material as new material comes in. You need to stay hydrated. Go online to the NACHO chat list and read some of the ways people are staying hydrated. It's a big issue, and a big step toward getting over the natural cleansing energy let down.

3. You're going too long between juicing and meals. You are starved for calories and blood sugar, and as every person who has successfully lost weight knows: **the fastest way to failure is to get hungry.** Read that again. Write it on your hand and your car mirror and your computer monitor: if you're having a hard time with this cleanse, it's because you're not planning your eating schedule well enough. You're still on automaton with your thinking about food; you're doing your food thing the *same way you've been doing it for decades.* You'll find yourself caught on the freeway, or sitting in your office, and your blood sugar levels drop, with not a freshly squeezed juice or good food in sight. This blood sugar drop leads to depression, to low self esteem, to thoughts of "see, I knew I couldn't do this, I'm too dang busy", and since the candy machine down the hall, or the "food" at the local gas station doesn't contain fresh squeezed celery-carrot juice, you give up, give in and wake up ten minutes later half-way through a chocolate bar.

All success on this cleanse requires breaking with old habits and the old ways of doing things. And most importantly, bringing attention to areas that were heretofore asleep. Any habit is a place where we are asleep, and this cleanse requires rethinking and being aware in the world of food.

Creating a network

In my own life experience, most of what I know I have learned by example, by modeling others. My heroes are all people who went through some experience and came out the other side to teach me what they discovered first hand. Not theory, but actual experience.

This kind of actual experience is invaluable when you enter the world of self-regenerative health. I cannot emphasize this point enough: when you personally hear from someone who has reversed a symptom, been through cleansing and understands how it works, has seen a skin problem improve, found more energy, knows of people who feel better, and they can tell you how they did it, then the desire and motivation to experience this yourself becomes real.

Those who post messages and their results on the NACHO Forum (http://www.howhealthworks.com/forum/) are generally not medical professionals. They are lay people, from all walks of life, who have found success in using this program, and have a passion for helping others to experience the same. They can give you their own experience, and share the network of others who are part of this movement to bring common sense back to our understanding of health. They can give you ideas for accelerated results. And perhaps most importantly, they can help raise your standards and keep you on track with your goals and commitments that you made to yourself.

What Next? After Your NACHO Cleanse

It's the evening of the 28th day of your NACHO cleanse. You've reached the last day. *You made it.* You actually stuck through four solid weeks of a nutritional cleansing program, something only a handful of humans can say that they have done. You persevered through some emotional, physical, psychological, and maybe even spiritual hurdles. You stopped eating by **habit,** and started eating by **thought**—actually thinking about what you were feeding yourself.

Well... what next?

Here's the first suggestion, and I use the word "suggestion" carefully: tonight, go celebrate. Go eat and drink and consume exactly what you were fantasizing about during those first couple weeks. Pig out. Order chips and beer;

two martinis; eat white flour products with cream sauce; order a barbecued steak; eat sugar; consume a pint of ice cream, right out the container; have a double espresso, followed by your favorite diet soda or cola. Whatever your heart desires. Enjoy the evening, savoring the gustatory orgasm of taste, toasting your success, feeling what free will and freedom of choice feels like. You deserve a night on the town, with no constraints, no guilt, no holds barred. Have a blast.

Then go home and go to bed.

The following morning, I want you to do me a favor: **write me an email.** Address it to Info@howhealthworks.com, and describe for me two things:

• **First, examine how you are feeling, post cleanse and post party.** Compare this morning's overall sense of well being with the last few mornings. Note any changes in areas such as brain function; amount of overall mucus being produced by your body; the quality of your breath and the coating on your tongue; the way your skin feels, maybe any itching or skin coloration; any difference in body smell; color of your eyes; consistency of your bowels; and overall energy level. Just note how you feel, compared to yesterday.

There is a reason for suggesting this all out celebration meal. The most obvious is for the contrast: you cannot create a more sharply felt, black-and-white comparison for what author Steve Gagné calls the *energetics of food,* than the time immediately following a nutritional cleanse.

This comparison is critical. It firmly sets in your mind, your beliefs, and your physical body the unmistakable yet socially underrated power of the effects of food on health and disease.

Remember, the main purpose of this book is to create a movement for nutritional sanity. This movement will not happen through intellectual discussion about the wrongs of selling McDonald's in school cafeterias. It will only happen through enough people having the physical experience—the oh-my-god, I get it!— AHA that comes from feeling the effects that our modern diet has on our health. Think for a moment of the organization called MADD— Mothers Against Drunk Drivers. Their single purpose was to wake Americans up to the bloody, horrible truth about drinking and driving. The founders knew that while most Americans intellectually understood the dangers of driving drunk, many people still did it with a wink-wink, cavalier attitude. It took a group of people who had had the actual experience of losing family members to drunk drivers—to shift that attitude forever. They forced a nation to grow up.

This cleansing program—and its contrasting follow-up no holds barred celebration meal—is designed to do a similar thing. It is to form a group of people, scattered all across the country and communicating online with each other, who have had the experience of cellular regeneration and "get" the effects of food on health. In a nation that has the immature, childish belief that "we are not responsible for our sicknesses", this has the potential for transforming the fabric of our world. It is time we grow up.

There is another reason, though, for the all out celebration meal: it is to remind us of free will. Life isn't just about eating foods that are cleansing and have "good for you!" smiley face labels stuck all over them. Life is for living, and that includes our nutritional choices. Our body has an amazing ability to handle a wide array of food and gustatory experiences without falling apart. There is so much glorious room to move around and experiment and play in the realm of food and cooking. The key is understand the limits, of recognizing the signs of too much of a good thing, and knowing how to return to base camp, to that place where you can reset the default button on cellular function.

And now you know how.

• **The second thing I want you to email me** is some thoughts on your overall process during your NACHO cleanse. What motivated you to try out a cleansing program? What was the hardest part, and how did you get through that? What classic cleansing symptoms (see the *Symptom List*, from an earlier chapter) did your notice? What changes have you seen? And most importantly, what insights do you now have about the whole process?

Have fun with your new path of health. And above all, have faith in the self-correcting, self-regenerating ability of your body. Once you understand what it needs, it will show you precisely how health really works.

Scott Ohlgren

To me, optimum health is a result of our ability to digest everything! Food, water, air, people, places, things, conversations, ideas, experiences.

Everything.

Russell Mariani

Medical Disclaimer

If you were born in or currently reside in America, it is important that you read the following medical disclaimer. Strangely, all other countries are exempt.

It is always best to consult a physician/prescription drug provider before undertaking any major shift in your diet.

This book, and the program described herein, are nothing more than opinions or suggestions, and are therefore protected under the First Amendment of the United States Constitution, which grants the right to discuss openly and freely all matters and viewpoints.

These viewpoints should not be used for the diagnosis or treatment of any ailment. Nothing said, or hinted at being said, or imagined being said, or told by a psychic that the author said, should be construed as medical advice.

None of the writers of these viewpoints can guarantee the accuracy or completeness of any information conveyed. The absence of a warning for a given vitamin, mineral, herb, plant, street drug, diet soda, Swenson's Frozen Dinner, or any combination of these substances should not be construed to indicate that the substance combination is safe, appropriate or effective for any given consumer. In particular, in no event will NaviQuest Corporation, How Health Works™, Scott Ohlgren, family members both living and dead, or ex-girlfriends going back as far as 1972 be liable for direct, indirect, special, incidental, secondary, or consequential damages resulting from any application of these viewpoints, even if advised that the viewpoints are good for you (examples of advice: "Eat this…" "We suggest…" "The sky is falling…"). If you have questions about your health care or another person's health care, please consult your physician/prescription drug provider.

All of the information contained within this written and audio material, suggested websites, or any related data, is provided with the understanding that the information and its providers shall not be responsible to any person or entity for any loss or damage caused, or alleged to have been caused, directly or indirectly by or from the information, ideas, or suggestions. Your participation with any of these ideas is solely at your own risk. **If the concept of "your own risk" and "personal responsibility" is not fully grasped, understood, and practiced in daily life, the writers of this material request that you do not utilize any of the suggestions laid out in this book. Instead, please consult your physician/prescription drug provider.**

Furthermore, if you are currently taking any medications whatsoever (prescription or over-the-counter), being medically supervised for the care and treatment of any illness or injury (especially the consumption of chemicals for "chemical depression"), scheduled for surgery, taking immune-suppressant drugs, or simply not sure what to do, please consult your physician/prescription drug provider.

The suggestions and opinions set forth are nothing but opinions, and should not be interpreted as anything but opinions.

The entire risk as to the results and performance of these opinions is assumed by you. If the instructions are defective, you, and not the authors, assume the entire cost of all necessary servicing, repair, replacement or correction.

This document contains no MSG, GMO seed stock, or other artificial ingredients.

No animals were harmed in the creation of this program.

Contents may be hot. Point away from face when opening. Do not plug into an outlet near an open body of water or bathtub.

Keep out of reach of children.

Do not induce vomiting.

Objects in mirror may be closer than they appear.

If you are pregnant or nursing... congratulations.

Resources

For a complete list of resources, please visit the How Health Works website.

SCHOOLS, ONLINE AND ON SITE

The School of Natural Cookery.

Since 1983, founder and author Joanne Saltzman (see her books below) has taught the art of cooking through true alchemy, versus "following recipes." If I was just starting out, this would be the school I would attend. Options range from short onsite intensives, to online classes. www.NaturalCookery.com 303.444.8068.

The Natural Gourmet Cookery School

Founded in 1977 by Annemarie Colbin (author of *Food and Healing*), this NYC-based school offers both public classes and a fully certified Chef's Training Program for a career in the rapidly expanding natural foods business. Visit www.NaturalGourmetSchool.com.

NUTRITIONAL COUNSELORS

Russell Mariani, The Center for Functional Nutrition

Russell Mariani is a Health Educator and Nutrition Counselor and has been in private practice since 1980, specializing in the prevention and correction of digestive system imbalances. The Center provides comprehensive information and support for the improvement of all health challenges.

For information about classes, seminars, retreats, and personal consultations by phone, please contact Russell directly at 413-536-0275; www.HealthEquest.com; 514 Amherst Road, South Hadley, Massachusetts, 01075.

Virginia Harper, The Ki of Life

Ginny Harper is the author of *Controlling Crohn's Disease,* Her own healing story is what has made her such a great nutritional counselor. Reach her at www.KiOfLife.com, (615) 646-2841, 106 Seminole Dr. Franklin, TN.

BOOKS TO WEAR OUT

COOKBOOKS

Romancing the Bean. Joanne Saltzman. If you want to learn how to cook for health, Joanne's books (and school) are the place to start. www.naturalcookery.com.

The Self Healing Cookbook, Kristina Turner. One of the

first books I ever wore out in the kitchen. Over the years I have purchased 30 of her books to hand out to friends.

Cooking the Whole Foods Way, Christina Pirello. Brilliant, modern, and complete. I love this book.

The Splendid Grain. Rebecca Wood. Rebecca is one of America's true compasses, pointing the way for our health and that of our children. Find her at www.rwood. com.

FOOD-DISEASE CONNECTION

The Cure of All Cancers, Dr. Hulda Clark. This is the first book to read if you have a life threatening set of symptoms. http://www.drclark.net/

There Are No Incurable Diseases, Dr. Richard Schulze. I have very few heroes, but Richard Schulze is one of them. He has a profound understanding of the diet/disease connection, and communicates with a no nonsense approach.

Food and Healing, Annemarie Colbin. My first health bible. I read this book four times, cover to cover. See her school at www.NaturalGourmetSchool.com.

The Energetics of Food, Steve Gagné. Gets you thinking about your "most intimate relationship." Purchase at www.redwing.com.

Edible Microalgae—A Review of the Health Research. Dr. Jeffrey Bruno, Ph.D. The Center for Nutritional Psychology http://www.nutritionpsych.com. If you don't believe the role that algae should play in our food chain, read this book!

Fats that Heal, Fats that Kill, Udo Erasmus

Pottenger's Cats, Francis Pottenger, MD, and *Nutrition and Physical Degeneration*, Dr. Weston Price. Both available through www.price-pottenger.org.

Dr. Jensen's Guide to Diet and Detoxification, and *Dr. Jensen's Guide to Better Bowel Care*, Dr. Bernard Jensen, DC. For the photographs alone, these two books will convince you of the power of cleansing, and motivate you to add years to your life.

Our Children Are... What Are Children Eat, Dr. Laura Thompson, Integrative Family Nutritionist. Few understand the connection between diet and child behavior better than Dr. Thompson. Call 800.608.5602 for her book.

Controlling Crohn's Disease, The Natural Way, Virginia Harper. If you know someone who has a digestive disorder, get them to read this book. It is a true story of the author's journey from near death to radiant health.

ANIMALS AND DIET

Most of our pets are eating the equivalent of canned meat and crackers. If humans don't do well on that diet, chances are good that our pets don't, either. Carol Bennett is a long time animal instructor and nutritional consultant who has mapped the diet/disease, diet/health connection. Author of *The Black and White of an Empty Harvest*, she can be contacted at www.animalconnectionnetwork.com. Email: acncarol@aol.com. Write her at: 2603 Delwood Avenue, Durango, CO 81301 970.259.4629

BODY HEALTH PRODUCTS

One of the more insidious ways we can poison the liver and weaken overall immunity is through the chemical laden creams, perfumes, shampoos, and deodorants placed directly onto permeable skin. As you become aware of the effects of these toxins, it often is increasingly difficult to hug those wearing chemicalized gland-based perfumes because of the toxin fumes that get left behind; I can smell those fumes for days on my clothes.

Chemicals accumulate in the human body, especially the fat and liver cells. You will often smell them coming out of your body during a cleanse, especially with the use of saunas and deep body work. Remember rule number one of cleansing: **Stop the Toxic Load.** One of the first places to do this is by examining what you are putting on your body in the pursuit of smelling, and looking, good.

Natural replacements to these body products are too easy. For underarm deodorant, try the enzyme-based one by *Kiss My Face*. In place of synthetic, gland-based fragrances, try Aubrey Organics, made from actual plants that grow out of the ground. I've used *Dr. Bronner's* liquid Castile soaps exclusively for over 23 years. For aftershave, hair spray, skin creams, etc., your local health food store can help you find nontoxic alternatives.

SUPERFOOD PRODUCTS

Cell Tech superfoods: I have used and recommended Cell Tech superfoods since 1988. They are the major farmers/harvesters of wild Aphanizomenon flos-aqua Blue Green Algae from Oregon's mountain Klamath Lake. I have toured their harvesting and manufacturing site many times over the years. Their stance for wild, organic, whole earth-based supplements make them one of the best sources for the superfoods and the Three Rs recommended throughout this book. To purchase their products, please contact your local distributor, or call Cell Tech directly (1800 800-1300).

Celtic gray sea salt: Contrary to what you might have heard, salt is still one of the basic starting points for human life. Unfortunately, we have confused salt with the sodium chloride that we all grew up with. The difference is night and day. To learn more about this distinction, as well as purchase the world's best salt, contact The Grain & Salt Society. Get a pound for the best price. Their website is www.celtic-seasalt.com, and their phone is 1800-TOP SALT.

Maine Coast Sea Vegetables. For alaria, dulse, kelp, and laver. Their Maine Coast Crunch wins my Best Sweet in the World award. I'd eat one every day if I could just keep them around. Their website is www.seaveg.com. (207) 565-2907. 3 Georges Pond Road, Franklin, ME 04634.

Mendocino Sea Vegetable Company. I've used John and Eleanor Lewallen's hand harvested sea veggies since 1985. Their Sea Palm is still my favorite in all the oceans, and the one I serve to seaweed virgins because of its great taste and texture. One of the best soups I ever made was based with their Fucus Tips Bladderwrack. And you haven't lived until you've soaked in a tub of healing Laminaria. Their website is www.seaweed.net. (707) 89-2996. PO Box 1265 Mendocino, CA 95460.

Rising Tide Sea Vegetable. www.loveseaweed.com (707) 964-5663.

EDUCATIONAL AUDIO/VISUAL

If you're doing the NACHO cleanse, I highly suggest getting the *How Health Works* educational tools, which as of this writing, have sold over 10,000 units.

The Three CD audio set:

> **1. Volume One, *Superfood Secrets,*** explains how damaging our current model of nutrition is, and using powerful metaphors and humor, shows us how to return to a sane approach to health. You will never forget "Digestion Dan"!

> **2. Volume Two, *Perfect Skin from Within,*** teaches us where our skin really comes from, and why it should be considered our body's largest elimination organ. Learn the "Five Bad Boys of Skin" and how to eliminate them.

> **3. Volume Three, *The Seven Physical Transformers,*** describes seven deceptively simple methods to increase and speed up the results you will get during your 28-day cleansing program, including sauna rounds, alkalinizing baths, skin brushing, and more.

The live video:

> The *Cellular Cleansing Made Easy seminar video.*
> If you can't attend one of the live *How Health
> Works* events, you can view it in the comfort of
> your own home. Includes inspiring testimonials.

See the www.howhealthworks.com for current pricing,
or email us at sales@howhealthworks.com. Volume discounts are available.

Water and Salt: The Miracle Medications (video) by Dr.
F. Batmanghelidj, M.D. This two hour video program
is presented by the world's number one authority on
the healing properties of water and Celtic grey sea salt.
Contact: www.watercure.com.

Scott Ohlgren is an enthusiastic student, teacher, and beneficiary of the natural healing paradigm. Periodic cellular cleansing has been a central part of his life for the past 20 years and the main reason why he hasn't used a single antibiotic or prescription drug since 1976. His writings have appeared in the Bay Area Monthly, Cell Tech International, Grain & Salt, and he has sold over 14,000 tapes, videos and books on the diet/disease connection. His first book, The 3Phase Manual (now out of print) sold over 68,000 copies.

Scott is a 1985 Kushi Institute graduate, a nine-month intensive live-and-study program on food sciences. He studied at the Rolfing Institute and became certified as a Rolfing Practitioner in 1988. He is board-certified by the American Association of Drugless Practitioners as a Holistic Health Practitioner, and is accredited by the Florida International University for CEU credits.

Scott's mission is to create the La Leche League of nutritional understanding. His passion, which is obvious in his videos, tapes, and live events, is to have people prove to themselves—to have the physical experience—of this connection between their current symptoms and the food that they have been eating for decades. To show that the role of healer belongs not to those "from hospitals or laboratories," but is actually as close to home as hand to mouth. It then becomes apparent that our job — as parents, teachers, and leaders—is to return the responsibility for our health back to where it has always belonged.

To bring the HHW lecture to your area, school, or group—or to learn how you can present the principles taught in this book— contact his office, at info@howhealthworks.com.

Scott and his wife, Gael, live in Boulder, Colorado with an outside sauna and cold plunge, as well as a couple of cats and a dog. His next acquisition will be a goat, to mess with the dog's mind.

Index

If you would like to have the How Health Works seminar come to your area, school, or group—or are interested in learning how to teach these principles yourself—please email us at info@howhealthworks.com.

Discount Order Form

This order form is for the two main 28-day cleanse items:

    1. The *Cellular Cleansing Made Easy* book

    2. The 4-piece book/3CD audiobook educational combo

Fax orders: 303 527-0270

Email orders: sales@howhealthworks.com

Postal orders: 7440 N. 49th St, Longmont, CO 80503-8847

Prices:

Cellular Cleansing Made Easy
1 copy: $14.95 • 2 copies: $12.95 ea. • 5 copies: $11.95 ea.

4-piece book/CD audiobook combo
1 set: $34.95 • 2 sets: $29.95 ea. • 5 sets: $24.95 ea.

Name: _____

Address: _____

City: _____

State: _____ ZIP: _____

Telephone: _____

Email: _____

Visa/MC: _____

No. of books: _____ x $_____ = $ _____

No. of AV Sets: _____ x $_____ = $_____

Shipping: $4.00 first item/set, $1 each additional: $ _____

Total of this order: $_____

Each 4-piece combo contains: 3 CDs, *Real Food, Real Health* (*Superfood Secrets, Perfect Skin from Within,* and *The 7 Physical Transformers*) and the book, *Cellular Cleansing Made Easy.*